Unequal Access

Women Lawyers in a Changing America

Ronald Chester

foreword by Cynthia Fuchs Epstein

BERGIN & GARVEY PUBLISHERS, INC.
Massachusetts

This book is dedicated to:

Those who struggle

Library of Congress Cataloging in Publication Data

Chester, Ronald, 1944–
Unequal access.

Includes bibliographical references and index.
1. Women lawyers—United States. I. Title.
KF299.W6C46 1985 340.023'73 84-9355
ISBN 0-89789-052-3

First published in 1985 by
Bergin & Garvey Publishers, Inc.
670 Amherst Road
South Hadley, Massachusetts 01075

56789 987654321

Printed in the United States of America

Contents

Foreword

The 1920s were regarded as a time of emancipation for many Americans. World War I had been won, women had attained the vote, and the mood of an open society, one freed from restraint, was marked by a rejection of traditional behavior. In this context, a small number of women began to attend law school. Some were seeking a profession to support themselves, some wished to help out in a family firm or business, and some sought to improve their lives. Many were unaware that the legal profession was far from open to women or members of minority groups.

Ronald Chester's fascinating account of the women who went to law school in the 1920s and 1930s chronicles through oral histories the experiences of people doubly and triply disadvantaged. Society promised them opportunity through professional training but restricted it to a limited number from "acceptable" backgrounds. Men who attended non-elite law schools at night had problems getting good jobs as lawyers, but women faced almost insurmountable barriers. Chester has captured the spirit and fortitude of a sample of women from lower middle-class and working class families, who overcame these barriers. Their voices can be heard through the case studies that make up this book.

Some of Professor Chester's conclusions, based on his interviews with these women, sound amazingly contemporary. Women lawyers of the 1920s and 1930s, like young women lawyers of today, felt that they must work harder than men to prove themselves. Many, also like the young women of today, refused to acknowledge discrimination. Eyes on their targets, they looked ahead and worked hard. It may surprise readers to find that networking among women is not a new phenomenon but was practiced by those early law school graduates. In fact, quite contrary to common belief, women attorneys who were fortunate enough to get jobs made it their business to help other women—then as today. There are no tales of "Queen Bees" in these accounts. To the contrary, networking organizations such as the Women's Bar Association of D.C., the Women Lawyers Association and the Kappa Beta Pi Legal Sorority in Washington, D.C. made it possible for many women to find employment. Often it was not as a lawyer; rather these women lawyers had to be content with jobs as legal secretaries, but they did help each other find work with legal content. The few women who had contacts and power were generous in using it to the advantage of other women. Take the case of Annabel Matthews, who, as Chester reports in detail, fended off male candidates for a post in her office at the U.S. Board of Tax Appeals with rejection letters that stated: "I have not yet appointed my second legal assistant, but I expect to select a woman lawyer."

As I reported in *Women in Law,* Chester shows how prior to the 1970s women lawyers tended to work in "protected" sectors of the Bar, in practice with husbands or fathers, or in government service. The clustering of women in government service made networking particularly effective in Washington, D.C., one of the locations in which Professor Chester did his research. Women needed all the help they could get. Even the "open society" of the New Deal did not prove to be open to them; many women lawyers had to take secretarial or clerical positions in government at the time. Chester augments the oral histories of the women attorneys in his sample with important empirical information such as the fact that no women at all were examined by government agencies for the professional grades of associate, junior or senior attorneys in 1930 or 1938. Only in one year during this period—1935—do the figures show women in government attaining professional rank as lawyers. Nevertheless, women law graduates found work in government (if without professional rank) because they were aided in their search by the informal network of female attorneys that he describes.

In the 1960s and 1970s I studied women lawyers who had gone to a wide array of law schools. Even those who graduated at the top of their classes from the most prestigious schools continued to encounter resistance from law firms although by then government had become a more accessible route to a legal career. Many women lawyers gave up legal careers, as we see from Chester's sample. A portion of the "survivors" finally were able to develop careers but only after the anti-discrimination legislation of the 1960s began to be implemented. It still remains difficult for graduates of the less prestigious schools, particularly the night legal programs, to achieve the equal opportunity promised by our society.

By revealing the severity of the problems women attorneys have faced in the past, Professor Chester has shown us how much we can learn about the enduring prejudices against women in the legal profession. In this work, like his other important contribution to the literature on the gatekeeping activities of privileged groups, *Inheritance, Wealth and Society,* Chester has fleshed out the picture of how barriers in society deny equal opportunity to otherwise eager, hardworking and aspiring groups—in this case, women. He has done so in the dramatic and convincing words of women who confronted prejudice at a time when it was both legal and accepted in American society. Their experiences, long neglected, speak to us vividly despite the years that have elapsed.

—*Cynthia Fuchs Epstein*

Preface

In January of 1981 at the annual meeting of the Association of American Law Schools in San Antonio, I had discussions with Prof. Martha Fineman of the University of Wisconsin Law School which led to the creation of this book. For years I had been interested in the history of my own law school, which had operated from 1908 to 1938 as Portia Law School—the only all-woman's law school in the world. My work to date had concentrated on the achievement of equal opportunity in various aspects of American life; discussions with Prof. Fineman and a number of legal historians at her law school convinced me that the study of women in law would lend a further dimension to this enterprise. There suddenly seemed every reason to study Portia and other working women's law schools, and to evaluate their contribution to women's participation in the American Dream.

Since I was a man seeking to write about women, I early decided that the best way of approaching the subject was to let the women who sought to enter the male enclave of law speak for themselves. In attempting an oral history of women who participated in the first rush of their sex into the profession, I realized I was sacrificing something: the neatness of history written with a single point of view. The result is a complex portrait of early women in law as they saw themselves—a result unlikely to please fully either strong feminists, or those who have viewed women in their more traditional family role. By selecting representative interviews out of the some 50 which were conducted, I have tried to give the reader the raw material from which to draw her own conclusions about the motivations of these women and the challenges they faced.

In attempting to make the interviewing as bias-free as possible, I was fortunate to have the assistance of Dr. Nia Lane Chester, a social scientist then at Boston University. Dr. Chester helped me devise the

Interview Protocol (sample reproduced in the Appendix) used by my student interviewers and me; she also trained us in interviewing techniques. Without her help and that of my two energetic assistants—Laurie Applefeld and Ann E. Rascati—this book could never have been completed.

Even with all this help, I doubt that such a book can be made wholly error-free. Anyone who has had the experience of transcribing interviews from tape knows the difficulty of the process. If any mistakes have occurred they are unintentional and I regret any misunderstanding—however slight—they might cause.

I have been asked a number of times why I chose to write this book. One of many reasons is reflected in a childhood memory. I recall occasionally accompanying my aunt, Janet, lobotomized as a young woman, as family members took her for her Sunday ride from the State Hospital. Janet had been a brilliant, beautiful, but it seems, incorrigible young woman, unhappy with the role into which life had cast her. She fell victim to a particularly foolhardy and vicious means of social control of talented and eccentric women. In some small way, this book is written in her memory.

At base, the book is a story of struggle. In most cases, the struggle is individual and private; but each effort mirrors the greater social drama of women, striving to enter a hierarchical and powerful profession. Since this is a profession that did not want them then, and is ambivalent about them now, it is a struggle which is not nearly complete.

Acknowledgements

In addition to those named in the Preface and in the book itself, other organizations and individuals have contributed in a significant way to the creation of this book.

Funding for the project was provided by both The New England School of Law and a Radcliffe Research Support grant. The latter grant is funded by the Mellon Foundation and is jointly administered by the Murray Center for the Study of Lives and the Schlesinger Library on the History of Women in America at Radcliffe College. The resources of the Schlesinger Library also proved invaluable in my research.

The New England School of Law, under the stewardship of the Honorable James R. Lawton, Chairman of the Board, and Dean Timothy J. Cronin cooperated in every way with a project that they knew would be scholarly in nature, and not a public relations exercise. Similar cooperation was received at Washington College of Law under the auspices of Dean Thomas Buergenthal and Director of Development Paul Purta. Chicago-Kent College of Law kindly opened its records to me at the behest of its dean, Lewis Collens.

The audio-visual staff at the New England School of Law and secretaries at or employed by the Law School also proved invaluable in the recording of the interviews and the typing of the transcripts and manuscripts. New England students themselves, particularly those enrolled in my Fall, 1983 seminar "Historical Perspectives on Women in Law" contributed numerous helpful insights. Finally, Cheryl Hoyt of Emerson College provided an extensive and useful critique of the manuscript.

1

Introduction

Most of us recall George Santayana's famous warning, "Those who cannot remember the past are condemned to repeat it."[1] For women who want careers in law, with access to the profession's most prestigious and powerful positions, these words are especially poignant now. Though the ranks of women lawyers have swelled, rising from 13,000, or 2 percent of the profession in 1970, to 62,000, or 12 percent of the profession in 1980,[2] the economic crisis of the early 1980's may threaten these gains. For answers as to how current women lawyers might respond, I have turned to history: to the life stories of the first significant wave of American women in law, which began in the 1920's.

The 1920's, like the 1970's, were a time of unprecedented opportunity for women. In those years they got the vote, gained access to all state bars, and began to serve on juries. Birth control became widely available, contributing to a freer sexual morality; women smoked, drank, and even cursed openly and in public.[3] It was a heady time for a woman. For the first time, if she wanted to be a dentist, she went to dental school; if accountancy suited her, then it was off to business school; if she wanted to be a lawyer, many law schools were open to her. Barriers everywhere were crumbling: "If you wanted to do something, you just went and did it."[4]

school; if she wanted to be a lawyer, many law schools were open to her. Barriers everywhere were crumbling: "If you wanted to do something, you just went and did it."[4]

The seeds were planted for destruction of this freedom by the splintering of the women's movement in the 1920's. With the right to vote won, the main group of those women who remained committed to reform subordinated the emancipation of women to the cause of social reform.[5] Instead of following Alice Paul and her National Women's Party, they became Progressives.[6] New organizations like the League of Women Voters were central to this persistent Progressive thrust.[7] At the same time, business and professional women rapidly acquired the attributes of professionalization. The National Federation of Business and Professional Women and the National Association of Women Lawyers became more attractive than traditional feminist groups. The social concern of educated women, and particularly their concern with women's rights, declined as their attachments to male-dominated professions grew.[8]

The depression of the 1930's halted women's progress in gaining access to business and the professions. During that period it was seriously suggested that married women be prohibited by statute from taking jobs if their husbands were employed.[9] Many of those who had begun to forget, in the eurphoria of the 1920's, that they were regarded by society as women first and professionals second were forced back into the home. This can be seen in the major revival of domestic industries, staffed by women, in the 1930's.[10]

While World War I had been "the first hour in history for the women of the world,"[11] World War II provided no such stimulus. Although women in all occupations rose 48 percent between 1940 and 1944, the gain was only 1.2 percent in the professions. Many women's jobs were "for the duration" of the war only, and the best jobs were saved for the men when they came home.[12]

As Betty Friedan has observed, the educated women of the 1940's and '50's (in contrast to the earlier generation) did not think to pursue careers, but sought fulfillment in home and family only. By some accounts, the proportion of women in the professions and professional schools actually declined until the 1960's.[13]

It is no secret that the Great Society of the mid-1960's, which produced equal employment legislation and contributed to the near-revolution of the late 1960's, brought the women's movement abruptly back to life. Women in the 1970's had all the freedoms of the 1920's, and more. In law, access to law schools and particularly to entry-level jobs in the profession was much easier. However, access to the "power jobs" in the legal and other professions remained uncertain.

Despite their new numbers women of the 1980's do not define the way our preposterously competitive, hierarchical, and expensive legal system is run. Nor, as obstetrician Michelle Harrison found in medicine, do they even define how the medical profession treats the problems of women's bodies.[14] The New Right movement that brought Ronald Reagan to power and helped to defeat ERA (first introduced in 1923) in the state legislatures can be seen primarily as a movement to "put women back in their place."

The "new feminism," which helped spawn the New Right backlash, recognized that suffrage had been only the first step. Now feminists concentrated on women's subordination within the family. Men were encouraged to share in child care and a number became socialized in this way, often pushed by the economic necessity of their wives' working. Easy birth control in the form of "the pill" and a change in attitude delayed families and made them smaller. Many women did not marry or, when they did, attempted to keep their own identity, career, and family name. Women in large numbers also began to perceive the professions as offering careers, rather than just jobs. These are far-reaching and rapid changes; one can readily understand the fear they engendered in most men and in more "traditional" women.

In law, these changes are having marked impact. Epstein reports that of women she interviewed on the eve of this "revolution" (1965), fewer than 10 percent of those in New York area law schools chose them on the basis of academic criteria. Practical concerns restricted their choice of law schools: pressure to be at or near home, desire to combine work with education, and a general emphasis on short-term non-career considerations rather than long-run occupational gains, planning, and goals.[15] These were similar to the concerns of the women in law school in the 1920's and 1930's.

In contrast, although some women in law school in the 1980's may have similar attitudes, the majority do not. Indicative of the fact that many women are now, like men, pursuing career goals, is that they are no longer overrepresented in less prestigious part-time legal education. In fact a slightly higher ratio of women to men now go to law school full-time, rather than part-time.[16] This is because many women in law school no longer wish to be restricted, as they were previously, to "women's work": family, government, public interest, and defender law.[17] Whether they will be able to break into the more powerful jobs (and perhaps transform them) depends in the first instance on their remembering that though they are individuals and professionals, they are—until society's attitudes are changed—women first.

THE STUDY: A TALE OF THREE CITIES

I came to this study with only a few preconceived notions about women in law. For one thing, I thought they had been denied equal opportunity in the profession. For another, I thought them as fit—or unfit, as the case may be—for the profession as men. I decided that I would let women in law tell me their own stories before I drew any conclusions. Thus, my first task was to set up a series of interviews.

In choosing whom my assistants and I should interview, I acted on my belief that we could best understand women in law today by studying the history of their access to the profession. Since, in the main, this is a story that begins after World War I, I resolved to interview women graduates of certain American law schools in the 1920's and 1930's. These decades represented, respectively, the period of women's first significant movement into the profession and a period when severe economic depression threatened what gains they had made. The women lawyers trained during this period would, I reasoned, provide us not only with a glimpse of the past, but with the perspective which the experience of a long life provides on the present.

Although a few women did attend non-urban university schools with full-time instruction, women in law of this era were enrolled primarily in urban law schools, particularly those with a heavy emphasis on part-time instruction. My own law school—then Portia Law School—was such an institution. I thus began the study by sending requests for interviews to all living alumnae of the Portia classes 1920 through 1939 who still lived in the Boston area. This was supplemented by a request for documents and information from those graduates of those classes who lived too far from Boston to make an interview practicable. Since Portia was a part-time law school, which served chiefly women of working-class and lower-middle-class families who had to work while attending school, I next used the same technique to study graduates of a full-time law school, Boston University. My hope was that the stories of the BU women would serve as a control on what I assumed would be the somewhat different experiences of women at a part-time school.

When I sought to expand the study outside of Boston, I began with a law school I knew about in Washington, D.C., the Washington

College of Law (now a part of American University), which was part-time, like Portia, and had been founded by two feminists. I used the same research method for WCL graduates as I had in Boston. In Washington I also interviewed a graduate of George Washington University Law School, which was primarily a full-time institution at the time. Since WCL women had come from many different states, often to serve the federal government, they were somewhat more representative of national trends than were the more provincial women who attended Boston law schools.

I chose Chicago for the final series of interviews, for several reasons. The first was a desire to see how women lawyers had fared in a city away from the Eastern seaboard. Since I had discovered in my Washington research that the first women's legal sorority—Kappa Beta Pi—had been founded at the Chicago-Kent Law School,[18] I resolved to start there. This school also fit that pattern so important to women; like Portia and WCL, it was an urban law school known primarily for its part-time instruction. Because, however, of the Midwest's greater support of public higher education, Kent's graduates, unlike most women at Portia and WCL, had one or two years of a college education. This difference turned out to have some significance for career patterns.

Naturally, some women during the period attended non-urban law schools, particularly in the West and Midwest; in these schools they represented a tiny minority in their classes. Since these women were often WASP, middle- to upper-middle-class "burghers' daughters," attending state university law schools which were essentially free—their stories would exhibit some differences from those told here.[19] I am confident, however, that theirs was not the main story of women in law in the 1920's and 1930's. That belonged to the urban, working woman of less secure socioeconomic and ethnic background who had to work her way through a private law school.

The concentration of this book on the urban bar and the urban law school with a part-time division sets it apart from other studies of women lawyers. Few of the women lawyers it discusses became very "successful," at least by the standards of their male-dominated profession. Although the standard work in the field—Cynthia Epstein's *Women in Law*—touches upon the lives of such women, they were not the primary focus of that book.[20] This instead is what may be thought of as a social or "people's" history. Most of its heroines are ordinary people struggling with the barriers created by a professional world that did not want them. As it is now commonplace to observe, discrimination against women or against other minority groups will be conquered only when "ordinary women" such as these have a place alongside ordinary men in various occupations, including law.

*****

A word should be said about my use of oral histories. I have tried to keep in mind in framing the narratives of those interviewed that their experiences are influenced by three major factors: (1) society, (2) culture, and (3) personality. Society influenced these women because of the physical fact that they lived among other human beings who had some power to permit them to do certain things and also to prevent them from doing others. Thus, statistics and other facts were used to set the framework for the interviews. Culture—ideas, knowledge, customs, values, and attitudes—influenced these women by enabling them to discern certain avenues of behavior and blinding them to others. Often I discuss what cultural influences were present in their society and often the women themselves discuss these influences. Finally, these women's individual personalities are important in shaping each one's response to cultural and social influences. Thus, the interviews themselves provide us with these people's idiosyncratic interpretations of outside influences.[21] Insofar as these personalities fall within recognizable categories, they can tell us what responses were most effective in the light of the difficulties and opportunities women faced.

Of course, what people say in an interview depends to some extent on who is interviewing them. Some of these interviews were conducted by me personally, the majority by two female law students working with me. Thus, where appropriate, I attempt to explain the effect that a particular type of interviewer might have had on certain responses. In all cases, we tried to remember that the interviewee was doing the teaching and that we were there to learn.[22]

In editing the interviews for this book, I have tried to maintain spontaneity in the language to allow the reader to better understand the person talking. Thus, though I might have chosen different wording for some of the ideas expressed, I have limited the "cleaning up" of diction, grammar, and syntax so as to avoid stilted and unnatural language.[23] In keeping with the informal nature of oral history, I have used the first names of the interviewees. To shorten the transcriptions and to avoid unnecessary intrusion of the interviewer's remarks, I have used a third-person narrative form, liberally interpolated with the interviewee's first-person responses. This method also allows some interpretation of the remarks as they unfold, although I have tried to do this only where it seems necessary for clarification.[24]

2

Women in the Bar of the 1920's and 1930's

Anthropologists tell us that the more dispersed and heterogeneous a people are, the less they can rely on shared customs to govern them and the more they must depend on an openly articulated and complex body of legal principles. This phenomenon has produced in the United States the largest population of lawyers per capita of any country in the world, a population that continues to grow. According to the U.S. Census, American lawyers account for one out of every twenty-eight workers who can conceivably be considered "professional or technical."[1] As of January, 1983 there were 612,593 lawyers in the nation.[2]

In addition to the influence attributable to its size, the legal profession is extraordinarily influential because of its intimate connections with politics and big business. Traditionally, the profession has also been extremely hierarchical in nature, granting women and minorities only very limited access to its more prestigious and remunerative positions. Instead of a single open and mobile profession, law in fact consists of several subprofessions, stratified largely on the basis of law school attended.

The first step for a group seeking elite legal jobs is of course entry into *some* level of the professional hierarchy. Women, for example, made up only 2.8 percent of lawyers at any level in 1970—a striking statistic.[3] Recently, however—and much more quickly than for other disadvantaged groups—things have begun to change for women. Between 1970 and 1979 women entered the law in such numbers that they constituted nearly 10 percent of the profession by the end of the period. Even more portentious is the increase in women as a percentage of all law students: from 3.4 percent in 1965, to 10 percent in 1970, and to a striking 30 percent in 1979.[4]

Thus, the 1970's have seen an enormous increase in the numbers of women entering the legal profession, a number that is growing exponentially in the 1980's. One is tempted to feel that once accomplished, this revolution is secure. Yet, as Mary Roth Walsh has shown for women in the medical profession,[5] this is not an assumption that should be lightly made. This book will trace the historical roots of this revolution both to uncover a little-known story and to shed light on women's future prospects in the law. In doing so, it focuses on the broader issues of the access of women and other disadvantaged groups into positions of genuine power and influence in our society.

*****

In 1880 there were only 200 women lawyers in the entire United States; which was less than the number of women doctors practicing in Boston alone.[6] In 1910 this number had risen only to 558, representing 1 percent of the profession;[7] in contrast, over 9,000 women doctors were in practice at the same time.[8] During the 1900–1920 period, however, it became easier for women to secure legal training, thanks to the growth of part-time law schools. The total number of women law students increased steadily, from 205 in 1909, to 609 in 1915, and to 1171 in 1920. In 1920 all states admitted women to the bar,[9] coincident with women's suffrage. Of the 129 law schools in existence in 1920, 27—including Harvard, Virginia, Georgetown, and Columbia—kept their doors closed to women.[10]

The same 1900–1920 period saw the closing of all but one of the twenty or so women's medical colleges and all medical schools offering part-time instruction. After 1910, the Women's Medical College of Pennsylvania was the only survivor.[11] This was important to the success of elite doctors and the American Medical Association in keeping out minority groups and reducing the number of women doctors.[12] In 1920 the number of women doctors in the country had been reduced to 7387.[13] Meanwhile, the number of women lawyers had shown slow but steady growth. Some have attributed the relative increase in women lawyers compared to women doctors to the delay of men's efforts to professionalize law.[14]

Though some in the American Bar Association and the Association of American Law Schools tried to close down part-time schools in the 1920's and 1930's, they failed.[15] The failure to keep out part-time schools was important to women, just as it was to other minorities. It appears that a large number of women worked either prior to or during the time they studied law, most frequently as clerical workers or teachers. Full-time training in the law schools often cost three to four times what the part-time schools charged during that period. Thus, because of lack of money, time, and college training, the majority of women attended part-time schools.[16] Others who had the time and money to attend the full-time schools often were denied admission on the grounds of sex; Harvard, for example, did not admit women until 1950.[17]

Nonetheless, the growth of the part-time schools encouraged the first great influx of women into the bar; this influx peaked in the late 1920's, their numbers in full-time elite schools was small indeed. The Depression stilled this boom in the 1930's; thereafter, the proportion of women lawyers in the bar remained nearly constant until the 1970's.

One part-time school, Portia Law School in Boston (now New England School of Law), was the only law school in the world to be organized exclusively for women. Founded in December 1908 by Arthur W. MacLean, himself a graduate of Boston University Law School and the law partner of Suffolk Law School founder Gleason Archer,[18]Portia was enabled to grant LLB degrees exclusively to women in a charter approved in 1919[19] by Governor Calvin Coolidge. It remained an all-women's law school at the LLB level until 1938.[20] The nation's only other women-only law school, Washington College of Law in the District of Columbia, followed a different route. Though founded "primarily for the education of women",[21] it was always coeducational and by 1937 was over three-quarters male.[22]

Law schools during the first decade of the 20th Century had widely differing programs, some extending only for two years.[23] Only about one-quarter of law teachers of the period taught full-time.[24] Like Suffolk and the YMCA Law School (now Northeastern), empowered to grant the LLB in 1904, Portia was largely a school for the children and grandchildren of immigrants. During the decade of its founding, lawyers with immigrant backgrounds rose 70 percent.[25]

A study done for Suffolk Law School in 1927 showed an ethnic composition that can be assumed to be similar to Portia's; one-half of the students were second-generation Irish; one-fourth were largely second-generation Jews and Italians; and the other one-fourth were mainly descended from poor, long-time New England residents of English and Scottish descent.[26] Similarly, the number of *foreign-born* lawyers in Massachusetts rose 80 percent from 1920 to 1930.[27]

During the 1920's and 1930's, Portia graduates, like those of other part-time schools, were quite successful in passing the bar. In 1924 82 percent of Portia graduates passed the bar;[28] by 1929 Portia showed a 65 percent pass rate compared to the overall pass rate of 40 percent.[29] Portia also showed the highest percentage pass rate among the three Boston part-time schools during the decade. Portia's pass rate in the 1920's was 46 percent compared to 41 percent for Northeastern, 38 percent for Suffolk, and 56 percent and 89 percent respectively for the full-time schools, Boston University and Harvard.[30]

The high bar pass rates of part-time schools were viewed with alarm by corporate lawyers in their role as leaders of the bar. Part-time schools were the home of "aliens, foreign-born citizens and native-born members of ethnic minority groups"[31] as well as women. "Armed with the weapons of higher educational standards and stringent bar admission requirements," these elite lawyers attempted to "purify their profession" of these alien influences.[32]

The imposition of higher standards was a two-edged sword. On the one hand, a more highly trained bar was necessary for the increasingly complex world of twentieth-century America. On the other hand, since Jacksonian times the law had served as a means of professional opportunity for ordinary citizens. By no means all of the profession needed to be as highly trained as its leaders.

As the economic crisis of the 1930's deepened, the suspicion grew that the elite bar not only was interested in higher standards but actively feared competition from the "ambulance chasers" pouring out of part-time schools. This suspicion was heightened when Massachusetts, like a number of other states, introduced an oral bar examination in addition to the written one. This "exam" involved a personal appearance by the applicant and focused on the discretionary criterion of "fitness to practice law."[33] Along with tougher grading of the written exam, this innovation succeeded in slowing access to the bar in a period of scarce legal business. Thus, in 1931 fewer than one-third of the takers passed the bar.[34]

In 1932 one Suffolk graduate, who had passed his written bar exam, ostensibly was denied admission because it was discovered on the oral exam that he was a plumber. This enraged Suffolk's Gleason Archer, who attacked the Board of Bar Examiners and its Harvard domination both on radio and in State House hearings.[35] In that year only 130 of 693 passed the bar. Still, Archer's charges of discrimination against part-time students were made in the face of the fact that 91 of the 130 successes were from evening or part-time schools. Ten women from Portia and six other women were among the successful.[36]

The bar exam was only one arena in which the conflict raged between the elite bar and their new competitors. The 1920's and 1930's were also a battleground in legal education itself. The chief protagonists were the full-time law schools led by Harvard's dean Roscoe Pound and a democratization movement led by Suffolk's dean Gleason Archer. In contrast to the experience in medicine, part-time law schools survived and flourished (although they sustained great losses of enrollment during the Depression); however, they gradually bent to elite admission standards.[37]

In 1920, Portia required only two years of high school for admission. Dean MacLean's figures for 1929 showed that 82 percent of his students had a high-school or college degree before admittance, 2 percent had a high-school equivalency certificate, and 16 percent had had some high-school training, making up the balance by graduation. MacLean decided that the 16 percent without a high-school degree could be replaced by men who had such a degree.[38] His petition to the Board of Higher Education to admit men was turned down, however, because his standards were "not high enough" for men.[39] Despite the opening of Boston College Law School, MacLean was able to find enough women high-school graduates to fill his classes, and by 1931 Portia demanded a high-school degree or its equivalent.[40] In contrast, by 1928 Yale had begun requiring a college degree.[41]

But the elite bar had not yet finished trying to "upgrade" part-time schools. In 1934 the Supreme Judicial Court of Massachusetts announced that two years of college training from an approved college would be required before the bar could be taken. Portia responded immediately by establishing a junior college, soon to become Calvin Coolidge College; in the same year Suffolk founded Suffolk College.[42] These were not high-quality institutions and did little to upgrade the educations of Portia and Suffolk students, who typically practiced in fields where the need for additional education was slight. Increased standards did delay their entrance to the profession, however, and allowed elite lawyers to pretend that theirs was a unified rather than stratified profession.

Despite the respite provided by these store-front colleges, both the part-time schools and their working students were hard hit by the Depression. Since it suffered under the added stigma of sex, Portia was affected most by declining enrollments. Finally, in 1938 Portia was empowered to admit men, one year after Suffolk had removed its self-imposed bar on women. The only law school exclusively for women in the world had fallen victim to economic hard times. At its peak in 1929, it was enrolling about 30 percent of all women in law schools in the United States.[43]

For one year during the first World War, Portia was confronted by another women's law school. Professor Henry Beale of Harvard founded the "separate-but-equal" Cambridge Law School for Women in 1915 with ten students. This "high grade law school for women . . . the only graduate law school for women in the United States," was heralded (in evident comparison to Portia) as "in no way a money making proposition."[44] Beale's law school folded after one academic year when his daughter, at whose urging the school had been created, lost interest.[45] Since the school took only women with a bachelor's degree, its market was severely limited anyway.

The story of the other women's part-time law school—the Washington College of Law in the District of Columbia—was strikingly different in significant respects from that of Portia. At its founding in 1896, no law school in Washington would admit women except Howard University, an overwhelmingly black institution. Two white women of some social prominence sought to change this situation. One, Emma Gillett, had attended Howard—somewhat, it seems, to her discomfort. The other, Ellen Spencer Mussey, was a member of the Washington bar and law partner of her husband, the well-known Washington lawyer General R. D. Mussey. She had apprenticed for the bar in her husband's office.[46]

Mussey and Gillett opened the doors to the Women's Law Class, as it was called, on February 1, 1896, in Mussey's own law office. Three women registered. The next fall, in response to embossed invitations, ten women and one man enrolled. Mussey taught Constitutional law and Gillett taught common-law subjects from Blackstone's famous treatise.[47] Unlike the amiable patriarchy led by Arthur MacLean at Portia, this Washington law school was run by feminists.

On April 2, 1898, the fledgling school was incorporated as Washington College of Law with Mussey as dean. Its articles of incorporation stated, "Primarily the college aims to provide such a legal education for women as will enable them to practice the legal profession." Indicative of Mussey and Gillett's social prominence was the acceptance by Edward F. Bingham, Chief Justice of the District of Columbia Supreme Court, of the presidency of the school's board of trustees. Despite its "primary" object, the school was coeducational, and one man, Paul Sperry, enrolled. He quit to become a minister after one year of study.[48]

In September 1898 the law school moved from Mussey's law office to its own quarters, adding three new lecturers to its existing complement of three. In 1900 an LLM program was begun, which conferred its first three degrees in 1901. That year's graduating class showed three men and three women. Since other Washington area law schools began admitting women after 1901, by 1914 Washington College of Law had more men than women graduates: twenty-five men, and twenty women.[49] This differential was to become more and more pronounced in the 1920's and 1930's. In 1936-1937, for example, 407 men and 124 women were enrolled.[50]

From the beginning, Washington College of Law was on shaky financial footing and depended on "leading members of the Bench and Bar serving at little or no recompense." That these individuals were willing to serve in this way, at least temporarily, was due in large part to the school's revolutionary aim of providing equal educational opportunity to women. In a 1907 grant application to the General Education Board in New York City, Dean Mussey stressed that Washington College of Law needed extra funds to put the school on a more business-like basis because "it is necessary to keep the tuition at a very low figure" to accommodate the school's working students.[51]

Until 1929, when it opened a small day division, Washington College of Law operated solely in the evening, on Monday, Wednesday, and Friday. The course of study lasted three years instead of Portia's four, reflecting the less stringent requirements of the District of Columbia Bar. Attendance was opened to anyone 18 years or older who had completed high school. Despite increasing pressure during the 1920's and 1930's to raise the latter standard, this was not done until the late 1930's. For example, WCL refused to change its requirements when Connecticut began demanding four years of college in 1929.[52]

WCL's resistance to higher standards for admission, like Portia's, stemmed chiefly from the financial need to fill its classes. A note from Dean Gillett to her Board of Trustees in 1925, although listing considerably more college work among her students than at Portia (40 of 84 applications for 1924–25), explained that this did not allow her to raise requirements to one year of college:

> Last year without a college requirement we had a deficit of $2,000 which was raised by discounts of notes by Mrs. Mussey and my-

> self. . . . I do not believe a small college like this can live in competition with large universities unless there is some advantage in its requirements for admission.[53]

WCL stressed the textbook and lecture system, combined with periodic quizzes, just as Portia did. However, perhaps in reflection of the school's more elite origins, more room was found for the Harvard case method. Casebooks were sometimes used and illustrative cases assigned to supplement textual study of "the more important subjects." Also in contrast to Portia, there was more practical training, including moot court and the use of legal forms.

Still, WCL, like Portia and Suffolk, was in the part-time school camp and knew who its enemies were. An editorial in the December 22, 1933 student newspaper attacked the August 29 speech of Harvard's Dean Pound before the American Bar Association's Section on Legal Education. The editorial opposed Pound's call for (1) a college degree for entrance (2) training in social science for lawyers, and (3) the teaching of general legal theories rather than local law.[54] An April 11, 1935 article in the same periodical noted with relish what it took to be a trend back to the more efficient textbook method and away from Dean Pound's cherished casebook approach.[55]

Although part-time like Portia's, WCL's student body was much differently constituted. The 271 students enrolled for 1929–1930 (less than half the number at Portia) came from 42 states and 10 foreign countries. The typical woman student (by now one out of every three students)[56] was a middle-class woman who had come to Washington as a clerk or secretary in government. Her family atmosphere would have had to be "worldly" enough not to impede her desire to work in the nation's capitol and in many cases to travel far across the country to do so. Students of every ethnic background flooded the school, but it is fair to say that its students exhibited far less concentration among second- and third-generation Irish, Jews, and Italians than did Portia's. Washington, unlike Boston, was a national city, drawing from far beyond the urban "melting pot."

During the 1930's, Portia's enrollment dropped, while WCL's showed a steady rise. This no doubt reflected the severe decrease in private legal business to which Portia graduates might look forward, and the sharp increase in national jobs which provided opportunity for WCL's graduates during the New Deal. Also, it should be remembered that WCL was now nearly three-fourths male; in a time of economic depression, a son's education was generally to be preferred to a daughter's, and that daughter, if seeking work or working, was less protected than her brother in a shrinking job market. In 1931–32 WCL showed an enrollment of 369, which increased dramatically to 605 by 1936–37.[57]

1938 was to be a momentous year for the Washington College of Law. As Portia's slow enrollment decline continued, WCL, which was by now bursting at the seams, faced a threat to its very existence. On July 1, 1938, the U.S. Court of Appeals for the District of Columbia abruptly changed its requirements for admission to demand two years of college training. After a great uproar, the Chief Justice interpreted the rule to be inapplicable to students who entered law school in 1938 or 1939 and who finished law school and passed the bar by July 1, 1943.[58]

WCL responded by raising its requirements to two years of college for the class entering in 1939. Needless to say this caused a great rush into the school in 1938, with 669 students enrolling that year.[59] The two-year college requirement at WCL allowed the school to apply for American Bar Association approval, which it provisionally received in 1940. Despite huge drops of enrollment after the new standards were announced (only 27 enrolled in 1940–41 for a total enrollment of 257),[60] WCL was suddenly a nationally recognized school, with sound hopes for the future.

The contrast with Portia is instructive. Dean MacLean had responded to increased bar requirements in 1934 by adding Calvin Coolidge College, a "store-front" operation, and in 1938 by getting Portia's charter revised to allow the enrollment of men. Yet its competitive position had declined so much as compared to Suffolk that Portia trustees must have felt that it could not afford to "go national" with a two-year college requirement although that could have brought ABA accreditation. Although a revision of WCL's charter in 1938 had enabled it to establish a college (such as Calvin Coolidge), Washington eschewed this route and raised its own requirements for admission to national standards. This proved both a brave and wise thing to do.

At Chicago-Kent College of Law, adaptation to higher standards had come a decade earlier and had been accomplished more quickly. The Illinois bar had instituted a two-years-of-college requirement in 1924, and at first Kent's reaction was the same as Portia's. In that year, the school hastily established a junior college. However, in contrast to Massachusetts, Illinois already had a public higher education system in place, and the junior college was quickly found to be unnecessary. Needy students were preparing in sufficient numbers at the

University of Illinois and state teachers colleges to provide Kent with all the applicants it needed.

*****

This book focuses on the access to the legal profession of women law graduates in the 1920's and 1930's in the context of the boom-and-bust socioeconomic conditions of the time. Although admission to practice was usually still possible without law-school training during this period, the entrenchment of state bar exams made law school a necessary preparation. One sees several patterns of women's law-school experience during this time. The first is that of the middle- or upper-class woman with a college education, who was often admitted as one of several women in a full-time school. Both because of their background and because law school confronted them early on with the reality of male attitudes toward their professional aspirations, those who graduated were relatively successful. The second pattern is that of the working-class or lower-middle-class woman, whose numbers were far greater, but who, because of socioeconomic realities, generally was less successful. Because of its unique situation in the nation's capital, Washington College of Law, though a part-time school, occupied a position between these poles due to the relatively high social status of many of its women and their substantial, though not majoritarian, numbers in the school. As we shall discuss in our final chapter on Chicago, the Chicago-Kent College of Law exhibited, by contrast, Portia's working-class, immigrant pattern. Because of the Midwestern emphasis on public higher education, however, Kent's "ethnic" women lawyers were generally better educated than Portia's.

At this point, some general trends should be made clear. It appears, for example, that the feminist consciousness which led to women's suffrage in 1920 began to die out with the "return to normalcy" in the 1920's, at least in areas outside Washington, D.C. Women who went to law school in the 1920's and 1930's did so, for the most part, without the sense of careerism that characterized men. A substantial number never took the bar and even more never passed it. Many went to law school because it seemed interesting, and if they should take and pass the bar, it would provide them a flexible career, one which could be juggled with husband and children. A number of these women married lawyers or had other relatives with whom they practiced; this provided easy movement in and out of the profession. Most did not see themselves as competing with men; rather they practiced in areas in which men were less interested, including matrimonial and probate work.

Career patterns among women, to the extent they were different from each other, tended to follow socioeconomic lines. Many of the women who went to Portia, for example, were "working girls" in their late teens from immigrant backgrounds. The practices of those who established them, like those of men in the same socioeconomic group, tended to be in small firms, away from downtown areas. This route occasionally led to local and state politics, although women generally traveled it less successfully than did their male counterparts.

The Depression years of the 1930's made it very hard for women to get legal business. Some, particularly in Washington, found refuge in the administration of New Deal programs; others became housewives, taking occasional cases. Sometimes a woman, usually with an upper-middle-class background and a college degree, actually made it into big-firm practice or important government or academic work. The new opportunities for women that had opened up as men went off to fight in World War II vanished in the rush of career-oriented men who flooded the profession at the war's end. Women's tangential role in the legal profession continued until the upheavals of the late 1960's turned the society upside down, giving women both the incentive and opportunity to enter the profession in large numbers.

As a teacher of law students who include this new wave of women, I naturally wonder how lasting this revolution will be. I believe that some of the answers may be found by examining the first big influx of women into the profession in the 1920's and 1930's. Does their inability as a group to form a critical mass of influential women lawyers that could have provided the basis for progress in the 1940's and 1950's have meaning for women now? Or are things so fundamentally different in the 1980's that a return to the marginality they experienced in the profession is impossible? Some changes—such as widespread birth control, smaller families, and men being socialized to child care—are indeed major ones. However, unless women in great numbers reach positions of power, e.g., as partners in important firms, senior people in government, and tenured professors in law schools, the gains of the last few years may be less secure than is popularly thought. A crunch in employment is already under way; how successfully women in law and other professions will be able to weather this change is a central question for our society.

3

Boston: Women Alone in a Stratified Bar

BOSTON LAW SCHOOLS AND THE BOSTON BAR

In the early years of the twentieth century, the growth and influence of university law schools paralleled the expansion and power of corporate law firms. A law school hierarchy developed in which Harvard Law School and its emulators like Columbia and Yale trained aspirants to the professional elite, while night and part-time law schools prepared members of minority groups for careers in politics, business, and the non-corporate bar.

In Boston, the congruence of interest between Harvard and the Federal and State Street bar was particularly strong. In turn, the Boston Bar Association seemed to exist solely for the benefit of Harvard-trained State and Federal Street lawyers.

Into this comfortable male Protestant enclave poured the huge wave of immigrants from southern and eastern Europe who came into American cities between 1905 and 1914.[1] For many of them, and particularly for their children, access to the legal profession, with its close ties to politics, became an index of American democracy. In Boston between 1900 and 1910 the number of foreign-born lawyers increased by 77 percent, and the number with foreign-born parents by 75 percent. Despite the restriction of immigration during wartime, between 1910 and 1920 the number of Boston attorneys with foreign-born parents increased yet another 20 percent.[2]

Since two-thirds of those admitted to the bar by 1910 were law school graduates, these dramatic increases showed that the law schools were responding to pressure for easy professional access. But it was chiefly the new part-time law schools that fed the increase in lawyers of immigrant origins. Between 1890 and 1910 the number of day schools increased from 51 to 79, or 60 percent, while the number of night schools soared from 10 to 45, or an increase of 350 percent.[3]

The movement to limit access to the bar in Boston coincided with the rise in the night schools and the number of lawyers with foreign backgrounds who prepared in them. With the metropolitan bar growing rapidly, the issue of elitism versus democracy was squarely presented. In part, efforts to suppress the bar's growth expressed the hostility of a besieged Protestant culture toward the changing ethnic and social contours of American society.

Gleason Archer and Arthur MacLean graduated from Boston University Law School in 1905, when one in three of all law students in the nation already attended part-time schools. They were aware of the deficiences of such schools: part-time instructors, lecture rather than case method of instruction, inadequate libraries, and students often too weary from jobs to concentrate. Yet the young law partners quickly grasped the enormous market for such education and saw only the small YMCA law school just beginning to tap it. The time was right for Suffolk and Portia; Archer and MacLean divided up the market by sex and within a few years both schools were off and running.[4]

Archer and MacLean could make some compelling arguments for the education they offered. First, by making legal education accessible and cheap, they would keep the profession from becoming an aristocracy.[5] According to the dean of another night school, the part-time students were people "of heroic mould . . . a goodly race, full of enthusiasm, industry, perseverance, and that fine courage which scoffs at difficulty and welcomes the fray, confident in the ability to win success and reach the goal of achievement."[6] In short, they were potential ethnic Lincolns. Second, they demonstrated that American institutions were capable of offering the opportunity which would make people of varied backgrounds a part of America. Related to this was the argument that only by offering such opportunity could people of diverse ethnic and social backgrounds be socialized into the ways of American legal and political institutions.[7]

The Harvard professoriate and the elite bar refused to be convinced. They united on the question of higher educational standards before admission to law school and the bar. Self-conscious professionalism spurred the teachers, whose own self-esteem was augmented by higher standards for admission in their own institutions. State and Federal Street practitioners, fearful of the new competition, used higher standards as a defense of the elitism that enhanced their own stature. Thus did the Association of American Law Schools and the Section on Legal Education of the American Bar Association join forces. Their elite professors and practitioners dismissed the "absurd belief" that high educational standards were undemocratic or un-American.[8] Anyone who had the drive to make it, could do so.

Nativism and xenophobia reinforced these professional concerns.[9] The dean of one university law school enrolled "a very large portion of foreign names. Emigrants . . . covet the title [of attorney] as a badge of distinction. The result is a host of shrewd young men, imperfectly educated . . . all deeply impressed with the philosophy of getting on, but viewing the Code of Ethics with uncomprehending eyes."[10]

It was into this cauldron that MacLean and Archer now ventured. Archer, the more outspoken and dynamic of the two, had built the largest law school in the nation by the 1920's and had become the most prominent spokesman for the part-time schools. He seldom flinched in the face of his bitter adversaries, the university law schools led by Harvard Law dean Roscoe Pound.[11]

MacLean and his venture, however, started more slowly. His institution was all but abandoned during the war when MacLean, tired of giving the bulk of the lectures and perhaps even more tired of lending the school money from his own funds, offered to make a deed of gift of the school. No one was found, however, who was willing to assume the risk involved. Still struggling in the fall of 1918, ten years after its small beginnings, the school petitioned the legislature for the power to grant the degree of bachelor of laws. After nine months of efforts by students and alumnae, the bill was enacted and signed by Governor Calvin Coolidge after a unanimous vote by the Committee on Education, the House and Senate.[12]

Perhaps by temperament, but more likely because his law school bore an additional stigma, Arthur MacLean of Portia Law School was quiet and unassuming about his venture. With Suffolk's advent, MacLean had only been able to get permission to enroll women from the Massachusetts Board of Higher Education. His later attempts to reverse this were rejected by the state in 1928–1929.

No feminist, but a firm believer in women's aptitude for law study, MacLean ran his school as a benevolent patriarchy.[13] Unlike the first women's medical college, which had been established in Boston some sixty years earlier, Portia did, however, allow women into its professoriate and into lower levels of its administration. (Also, MacLean's wife, Bertha, took over as dean while Arthur was ill in 1923–24.)[14] MacLean's attitude seemed to be, first, that there was a market to be tapped, and second, that there seemed no good reason not to provide women with a legal education. Neither he nor his school would press for full inclusion in the highly stratified Boston bar. Theirs was a quiet, inconspicuous revolution: one geared so as not to upset further the establishment that controlled the Boston legal profession.

Indicative of the prevailing attitude at the school were the opinions of its most prominent female teacher, attorney Bessie Page, expressed in the fall of 1928:

> Equal rights for women is a phrase that makes a great appeal to many women, but I don't see why woman want them. . . . [It] sounds well in theory, but I cannot help but feel that women lose more than they gain by such legislation. Possibly I am old-fashioned, but when women put themselves on the same level as men, they lose those privileges that are dear to them, that men are only too willing to give them. I, for one, should hate to surrender my privileges, and I think other women feel the same way.

After citing various laws, Miss Page, Portia's most revered teacher, concluded that if women would only "acquaint themselves with our present laws, they would be a lot happier than they are worrying themselves with insistent demands for equal rights." The newspaper quoting her was quick to assure its readers that Bessie Page did not "lack feminity. Her curly, bobbed locks gave her an attractive and youthful appearance, and nothing about her suggests the woman trying to ape the man."[15]

*****

The oral histories of women in law in the 1920's and 1930's are often stories of personal courage in the face of enormous odds. At an institutional level, these stories track the struggles between the elite bar and its law schools and the democratization movement which challenged them. Minorities of all kinds, including women, are a vital part of this drama. On a societal level, their stories trace the efforts of women of the period to enter the legal profession, which is a part of women's struggle to enter the professions in general. Theirs was the first great wave of women entering law school, which peaked, with Portia, in the late 1920's. Although an important story, it is one that has been largely ignored. The experiences recounted here were chosen as representative and should be helpful in evaluating the current and more dramatic movement of women into the law and other professions.

PORTIA LAW STUDENTS

Mildred Salerno, Letitia Paraboschi, and the Class of '33

It was late September 1929, and although Mildred Salerno (pseudonym) did not know it, the prosperous world that had encouraged her to enter law school was about to come crashing down.[16] This evening, as on most, she was concerned that she would be late for class. A graduate of East Boston High School, Mildred strode quickly up the three front steps of a large brownstone, nestled among others on Mount Vernon Street, Beacon Hill. Over the entry, atop two Roman pillars was emblazoned the legend "Portia Law School"; Mildred knew it to be the only law school in the world exclusively for women.

As she entered the law school, she spotted the administrative assistant and secretary to the dean, May Mosher, bobbed blonde head awhirl, attending to student needs in her small office immediately to the left of the entrance. Beyond the office was a lounge. In the left-hand corner was a file cabinet, containing manila folders named, as Mildred knew, for each of the 500 or so students in the school, including her. As May Mosher had explained, to each folder was returned the students' marked exams, and any other information the school thought the students should have.

The textbooks Mildred carried in her briefcase were large 12" x 12" coral, soft-covered compilations of mimeographed class notes authored by the professors themselves. Designed to open and shut firmly, they could be loosened and flipped over as the professor covered the text. Mildred also carried a supplemental hard-covered book for her real property course. It had been written by a professor at Harvard and contained printed cases.

Hurriedly, she turned right through two interior pillars and ascended the graceful curve of a magnificent stairway. On the third floor she entered a large classroom, just as the 6:20 bell sounded. A minute later and Mildred would have lost credit for the class; four such late attendances meant no credit for the course. This was a problem for Mildred, as she worked for a bank in the market district that closed at 6 P.M. Her accustomed route was to run with the heavy briefcase up Hanover Street from the market, down Cambridge Street, and up Beacon Hill on Joy Street, to the school. In the winter, she found this a difficult journey indeed.

Usually called Mitsy, Mildred was a pretty, dark-haired young woman, barely 17. She wore her hair longer than was the style in the free-spirited 1920's. This reflected the conservatism of a working-class background (her father was a barber) and a family not long removed from Italian soil. She was well liked and quiet, as would be indicated on her graduation four years hence by the "Class Will," which bequeathed "to our intelligent 'little' girl, a balloon so that she may get up in the world to more easily reach the height to which the clever brain of hers [will] lead her."

But it would be a long time until 1933 for Mitsy and an even longer time until she could reach whatever "heights" awaited her. Upon graduation from high school in the spring of 1929, she had been awarded a fifty-dollar scholarship by a women's club. The money was to be sent directly to whatever school she enrolled in; if she had not come to Portia that September, Mitsy would have forfeited the scholarship.

She had decided to enter Portia while working in the bank that summer. At the end of August, not knowing where to use her scholarship, she met by accident a friend, who had graduated with her from East Boston High. She told Mitsy that she was going to enroll at Portia, and Mitsy decided on the spot to do the same. The following week she registered at Portia, determined not to lose the scholarship. The fact that Portia was an all-woman's school, and therefore unique, meant little to her. In 1929, fifty dollars paid one-fourth of a year's tuition, and Mitsy was determined not to waste it.

Classes this September evening, as in each of the three evenings a week over the academic year, lasted straight through to 9:00 P.M. They were absolutely silent except for the professor lecturing from the bound class notes. Students were permitted to question the professor only after raising hands and being called upon. Though she was only dimly aware of it, Mildred was being taught by the "black letter" method, which was widely employed in part-time law schools. Her dean, like others in such schools, had reasoned that the "Socratic" question-and-answer method used at schools like Harvard took too much time for their classes of working students.

Even so, Mitsy had little time in her busy life. Immediately after classed ended at 9 P.M., she went to the school library, where she stayed until close to 11 P.M. There she worked on problems for the next class period. These gave a set of facts and asked for her interpretation of them, her application of the law involved, and finally her solution and the reasons for it. Since she worked six days a week until 6 P.M., the only other time she had for studying was on non-class nights, or on Sundays, which she spent working either at home or the Boston Public Library.

Arriving home that night at 11 P.M., Mitsy tried to eat supper, but, as on many nights, she could not force it down. Though she had not eaten since noon, she fell immediately into bed, exhausted. The next day was also a class day and she needed sleep more than ever. Social life was for other people. Mildred Salerno, uncertain a month before about her future, now reached back for the courage her future suddenly demanded of her. She would not know the meaning of "Depression" until later that fall; nor could she suspect that at the end of her four long years of school, this crisis would continue to becloud her future.

*****

Mitsy's class of 1933 had a day division as well. Also designed to accommodate women with other responsibilities, it met for three hours early on Monday, Wednesday, and Friday mornings. Letitia Paraboschi[17] was one of its members.

Letitia was nearly 40 when she entered Portia in September of 1929. Her husband, Cesare, was a lawyer, who had a small practice combined with title examining and who also worked part-time as an assessor for the City of Boston. Cesare thought it would be a good idea for Letitia to study law since their two daughters were in Girls' Latin School and thus almost surely college-bound. In case something happened to him, Cesare reckoned, Letitia could then help the children get through college.

Letitia and two other classmates were among the older students at Portia and became good friends. The others were (Mrs.) Alice Cunningham Lacey of Jamaica Plain and Ann McLaughlin of Woonsocket, Rhode Island. Lacey had also graduated from Girls' Latin and had attained a B.A. from Radcliffe and an M.A. from Boston University before attending Portia. Her background and maturity contributed to her election as president of the class of 1933 for three of its four years. McLaughlin, who had attended the New England Conservatory of Music, served as class vice-president for all four years.

Letitia was a quiet and serene woman who left class leadership to her better-educated friends. Like Ann McLaughlin, she spoke little—when she did, her conversation was short and to the point. Alice Lacey was the social one of the trio, combining dignity and grace with an ability to study faithfully. She was to remain Letitia's close friend until their death two weeks apart in 1981.

Letitia's life at school was considerably more settled than that of Mitsy, her far younger counterpart. At home her family, including Cesare, all cooperated in the various tasks of the household. Each night the family settled down to their books without the distraction of modern media. Only in 1931 did they acquire a large radio-phonograph, on which they listened to the Saturday afternoon opera.

On winter evenings the Paroboschi family first washed the dishes, and then usually skated in the back yard before beginning the evening's studying. In contrast to Mildred Salerno's spartan existence, Letitia entertained company nearly every Friday or Saturday evening; the Paroboschi home was always open to friends, and the friends reciprocated. School vacation meant dinner in town and attendance at a play, movie, or opera for the entire family.

The home was full of music and laughter. Cesare studied voice; Letitia taught her daughters piano. She also made many of the children's clothes. In the summer, all helped in the garden and in redecorating their old home. The Paraboschis became experts in painting, paperhanging, plumbing, and carpentry.

Letitia found Portia's schedule ideal for coping with her busy and close family life. She often remained at the law school or State House Library until midafternoon, and then went home to tend to her daughters. She graduated on schedule in 1933, the same year one daughter finished Girls' Latin and joined her sister at Radcliffe. Both daughters graduated from Radcliffe with honors, the first marrying an astronomer, and the second becoming an English teacher, head of department, and assistant headmaster in a large Boston high school.

Letitia Paraboschi had prepared herself for a career which she might not have needed, while maintaining and strengthening the family ties she valued so highly. Since Cesare lived to see his daughters settled—one well married, the other with a good career—Letitia never took the bar exam or practiced law. From time to time, she helped Cesare in his title examining, but illness in her immediate and extended family drew her attention away from law. By contrast, her good friend Alice Lacey, who married but had no children, actively practiced law. So did Mildred Salerno, although she was to give up much of it when she turned to marriage and family in 1938.

Letitia Paraboschi is as much a part of a book about women in law as either Mildred Salerno or Alice Lacey. All three came out of a part-time law school, shunned by the likes of Harvard and Columbia; all were women in a profession completely dominated by men; all were facing a bleak economic situation, in which even male lawyers found survival difficult. Generally, theirs and the other stories I tell in this book are stories of struggle in ordinary lives.

Jacqueline Guild: Black Woman Pioneer

Jacqueline Guild's story contrasts with Mildred's and Letitia's in significant ways.[18] Guild was born in Cambridge; her father was a lawyer and solidly middle class. Although she attended only Cambridge Latin School before entering Portia, both of her brothers graduated from Harvard College, one eventually becoming a doctor, the other entering government service with the Department of the Interior. Though of a more established family than many of her classmates, Jackie Guild bore a handicap which they did not: like a handful of others at Portia, Jackie Guild was black.

Jackie's father had graduated from Suffolk Law School and was for a time president of the Suffolk Law School Alumni Association. Very active in state and Cambridge politics, he eventually became Assistant Attorney General for the Commonwealth. He and his wife had both grown up in Boston; he had attended the Boston Latin School, where he was a classmate of Joseph P. Kennedy. One of his sons attended school with John F. Kennedy. In fact, John Kennedy and his sister Patricia occasionally visited the Guild household.

Jackie Guild never doubted that she would be a lawyer like her father. In those days of new freedom for women, she recalled, "It was amazing. If a woman wanted to be a dentist or a lawyer, she just went [to get the training]." Jackie's environment spawned little talk of a woman's place being in the home, even though her own mother was in charge of four children including her. Either professional or family options were encouraged; Jackie's only sister became a housewife like her mother before her, raising five children, while Jackie became the third black woman to pass the Massachusetts Bar.

For the first two years, Jackie went to day school at Portia. Her father, however, lost all of his money when the banks folded, and Jackie had to transfer to the night school and take a daytime job. Since she had done well at school, Portia helped her with a scholarship. Her days were spent cleaning up after a hairdresser in a Newbury Street barbershop. Her evenings were spent like Mildred's in class in the brownstone law school at 45 Mt. Vernon Street.

The school was handsome and comfortable inside, though somewhat small for its 500 to 600 students. Classic staircases connected the first three floors, all of which had wide fireplaces. The staircase to the fourth floor was much narrower, as was that to the fifth, whose dormers and low ceilings allowed only for storage. Large, open classrooms dominated three of the main floors, a library the fourth.

Dean Arthur MacLean, founder of the school, was one of Jackie's teachers. He was a handsome, trim man with sandy-brown hair, his wife a regal, distinguished-looking woman with blonde hair. They were not Jackie's favorite teachers. These honors fell to Chesley York, a prominent attorney who later became Massachusetts Attorney General, and to Bessie Page, the favorite teacher of most Portia women. York was a jolly man of heavy build. He was humorous and well-liked, characteristics shared by Dean MacLean.

Bessie Page was someone quite different. A graduate of Portia, Professor Page was a tall, very thin, gray-haired woman whom Jackie remembers as a brilliant teacher. She ran a popular bar review course for men and women graduates of the various Boston schools. A teacher rather than lawyer by instinct and desire, her concern for students was legendary. Although far less jocular than York, Page truly cared for her students as people. In Jackie Guild's case, this meant a free bar review course when money was tight for the Guilds in 1933. Jackie Guild was one of Bessie Page's best students, and Page wanted to make sure that Jackie started correctly on her legal career.

Throughout her school life Jackie belonged to the clique of serious Portia students—the ones who intended to become real lawyers. She was very popular and later claimed that she had never felt the sting of discrimination in school. Her best friend was Marion Dillon Gardner, who was somewhat older than Jackie and married. Marion had also gone to Cambridge Latin, but had then attended Boston University and Jackson College of Tufts University.

Marion Gardner lived in a striking house in Winchester on the Mystic River. Often she drove Jackie to her house, where the two studied together. Like Jackie, Marion was a serious student. Dark haired, with flashing brown eyes, she was known as a woman fond of both politics and the outdoors. In 1933 the senior class predicted that Marion would become a leading member of one of the strongest political machines in the United States. Like Jackie Guild's, Marion's four years at Portia were academically successful.

When Jackie Guild transferred to evening school, she became friendly with Rowena Taylor, another Cambridge High and Latin School graduate. Charming and well mannered, Rowena was not well known at school. She constantly seemed to be rushing back and forth to Cambridge in the service of her home and family. Eventually Rowena became solicitor for the City of Cambridge.

Jackie was aware that a number of her classmates were not as dedicated to passing the bar and becoming lawyers as she was. She attributed this to the fact that she had a place to go when she passed the bar. She knew she would step right into her father's law firm; the bleak 1930's held out no such prospect for most of her classmates.

"Schoolwork was hard," and Jackie felt that Portia was preparing her well. This feeling persisted in later years, when she fondly recalled her classmates doing "just as well" as the Harvard boys on the bar exam. Despite Bessie Page's efforts with the bar examiners, Jackie had to wait a year after graduation to take her bar exam because she was only 20 when she completed school in 1933. After successfully passing in 1934, she married immediately and then began to practice with her father. Unlike her unhappy black predecessor Jama White, who was expelled from Portia in September of 1926 and who sued the school for discrimination in 1929, Jackie Guild sailed right through, accepted and accepting. The fact that she was both female and black in a job market with little tolerance for either would not intrude until she tried to go it alone after a thirteen-year association with her lawyer father.

Sara Klier Wallace: Success Delayed

Sara Wallace graduated from Portia in 1930, overlapping Salerno, Paraboschi, and Guild.[19] Perhaps because her background led her to expect more of law school than they, her account of Portia is more critical, providing a darker side of the ledger for this unique school.

Sara grew up and went to school in Bedford, Massachusetts. Her parents were Poles who had moved to Germany and then to the United States as adults. She did very well in school and was strongly influenced by three unmarried women teachers: an English teacher (a

Radcliffe graduate), history teacher (Wellesley), and science teacher (Smith). Each wanted Sara to enroll in her college, perhaps as preparation for entering a traditional woman's profession like their own.

Sara's father was in the leather business, designing custom handbags. Her family had little money, and what there was was used to send a brother, some three years older than Sara, to college. He later became a chemist. A frail child, Sara was thought to be better off close to home. Her parents "didn't much care" what she did so long as she stayed nearby. Since one of her cousins from her father's family—Matilda Revel—was an early woman lawyer who had graduated from Portia, Sara followed her lead and enrolled. This choice was somewhat more to her father's liking than her mother's.

Matilda Revel had come from a well-educated but impecunious family who lived in the West End. Her own sister was a court interpreter for perhaps a dozen judges. Since there were few jobs, Matilda learned to be a title examiner "and did it for the best." After influencing Sara to go to law school, Matilda decided to teach Sara title examining too, so that Sara would be "employable" upon graduation.

Sara was very successful at Portia and, much to the relief of her parents, did not tax her frail health. She was the top student in the day class and won a small scholarship of about fifty dollars ("the only one they gave") in her first, second, and third years. During her fourth year (1929–1930), the Depression-threatened school gave no such scholarship at all, but Sara remained number one.

Sara remembered two general groups of students in the law school. The first group consisted largely of older women, many of whom were working as secretaries in law firms. "I think their goal was not so much to practice law as to better themselves in jobs that they had." For the most part they were very serious people "who worked all day and went to school at night." Some of them eventually did something in practice but most were not aiming for that. "The opportunity wasn't there, for one thing, and they just wanted the education to improve their possibilities for advancement."

The second group was very young, like Sara, who entered school at 17; most of them went to day school. Sara recalled that many of these women were not serious students. "They went to any place that was the place to go and was not an all-day school. I think some of them planned to take the bar, but a number did not." There were no admissions tests to determine whether students entering Portia had the ability to pass the bar, and "quite a few obviously did not."[20]

Of Sara's day classmates whom she knew, a few did impress her as serious. One she remembered was more than twice her age and headed the Catholic Social Service Bureau in a Connecticut community. As a social worker, this woman wanted to try her own cases when she graduated. There were also married women of varying ages, some of whom were married to lawyers. Most of these had not gone to college "and this was what they were doing to get ahead."

According to Sara Wallace, what a student got out of Portia depended on her. The teachers were "a mixed bag." Some were "not terribly good, but if you did your work . . . you did well despite the fact you weren't getting very good instruction." Many "just didn't have the background in education themselves to be teaching law." Exceptions were Bessie Page, of course, Professor William J. O'Keefe, who soon moved to Boston College Law School, and, to a lesser extent, Dean MacLean himself.

On the whole, the Portia law teachers were not good role models. "One didn't have very much to do with these people—it was a very part-time endeavor on their part, except with O'Keefe who wanted to be a full-time teacher." Sara had the most respect for him. Evidently, Portia also did not go out of its way to bring in prominent women in law to provide role models. She did not recall ever being offered the chance to attend a professional luncheon, which might have brought in a woman lawyer or judge as a model. "After you finished your 2½ hours of class, there wasn't much to keep you there." For example, the law library was so small that the women were encouraged to use the State House library a few blocks away.

Sara remembers other problems about Portia, problems not dissimilar to those of many law students before career placement became a "must." "Very frankly, you paid your tuition and went to classes. Whether you did or didn't find legal work afterward didn't matter much to the school. The school didn't feel any responsibility for its students." The students were not particularly surprised by this. "I don't think they expected too much of the school and so they didn't get anything."

The Depression lowered what expectations there were. The only ones in school Sara could remember as being very serious about continuing after the crash were the night school students. A number were working as assistants and secretaries in courthouses in outlying districts and expected to become clerks, which many of them eventually did. This was not Sara's goal; she wanted to practice law.

Sara graduated in 1930 and was one of a relatively small number of Portia students who took the exam in June of that year. Only thirteen women passed—exactly 100 fewer than passed the June 1929 exam. "I was first in the day class . . . assisting at that time Helen West Bradley who was giving the bar review course . . . I was informed that I was one of the top three scorers in the bar examination. Close to a thousand people took it and only 24 percent passed. The reason that there were so few passing was the Depression. It was a means of cutting the number of people practicing."

A woman friend of Sara's at Portia, who was "very bright" and a graduate of Regis College in Washington, did not pass the bar, but attempted to play a role in Sara's job search. "She was related to some very prominent people" in Boston, and through her brother-in-law, who was a judge, she attempted to get Sara a job. Potential employers "were interested," but it was absolutely impossible to get a job that would pay. They weren't hiring, and what they did do was take the recently admitted lawyers and give them some space and let them do some work, but there was no money . . . They were very nice, as perhaps they would be to one with Sara's outstanding record on the bar exam, but "things were very bad."

So Sara got part-time jobs correcting for the bar exam with Helen West Bradley and grading papers for Dean MacLean on constitutional law and contracts. "Otherwise I took an occasional case that I got through the publicity in the newspaper . . . [about her bar exam results. Nevertheless she would go to court] . . . on motions and things. . . . The clerks would come over [to the lawyer's enclosure] and ask me if I was a member of the bar. I married a doctor right after [graduation] and continued what I was doing, which wasn't very remunerative until my first child was born. It was impossible to get help because of the war, and I was home, and I had been doing a great [number] of community things. . . . I've been very active on my own."

"Community things" included a long term as president of the League of Women Voters and trustee at Childrens Hospital, where her second husband, a pediatrician, worked. Beginning in 1946 she served her home town of Brookline in various capacities, including president of the Community Council and advisory committee member of the first Redevelopment Authority. Later she was elected chairman of the Redevelopment Authority.

Meanwhile, Sara raised three children. When "my youngest went to Windsor School in Boston all day . . . I decided that I would go back and practice. . . . The selectmen asked me to work for them," and Sara has served from 1963 to the present as a consultant to the town, "doing some legal work" for Brookline. She was also quite active and successful in obtaining grants for Brookline for housing programs. She became a sort of compliance officer for the town with regard to civil rights and equal opportunity statutes. Sara was also a legal examiner for the town with HUD and the Department of the Interior, seeing that all town real estate "complies with regulations." In 1970, this pillar of the Brookline community was elected to the board of a "very conservative savings bank in town. That was nice," she recalls. Though her career has been an episodic one, interrupted by the Depression and childrearing, this talented woman from Portia has eventually become a central figure in the Brookline establishment.

Gladys Shapiro: Law and Politics as "One of the Boys."

Gladys Shapiro's life took a different tack, but she, even more than Sarah Wallace, became a "real lawyer" against formidable odds.[21] Gladys grew up an only child in the predominantly Jewish West End of Boston in the 1920's and early 1930's. "My people were in business, very well-known in the area. We were always very active in politics, and the political atmosphere pervaded my life from the very beginning. As a youngster I recall the political rallies. My mother was particularly active. She was a vice-president of the Women's Democratic Club of Massachusetts [the largest organization of its kind in America]."

Gladys's mother and father had been born in the United States, the children of parents who had emigrated from an area in Poland under Russian influence. "Both my parents were born in New York and emigrated to Boston. . . . My father came up in the same period of Mrs. Rose Kennedy. And they were neighbors. As a result he became rather interested in and close to the Kennedy family.

"My father went to Tufts Medical School, but he never completed it. My mother went to evening high school. In those days girls tried to work. She didn't get a high school diploma, but she had a lot of business acumen, and she probably would have made a better lawyer than I. . . . Instead, she became active in politics. She was a first friend of some of the outstanding political characters, such as Governor James Michael Curley.

"We were in the liquor business. My father had a package store in the West End. The family had been in this business since 1886, "as a result of which I became rather interested in the legal aspects of the liquor industry." Later on, after passing the bar, Gladys became a secretary of and counselor to the Boston Packagemen's Association, as a recognized specialist in the licensing field.

"Both my father and mother were active in promoting me to speak wherever they could. . . . The day I passed the bar my mother had a very expensive luncheon for me. It was held at the old Bellevue Hotel, and I was launched very nicely. I think every prominent politician in Boston was at the luncheon."

Gladys had begun thinking about that day when she was but 8 years old. She "had been reading some books about criminal law and that sort of thing. I was going to be a criminal lawyer, but [for the most part] it turned out differently" because of her interest in the liquor industry. Also influential was her mother, who was very friendly with Jenny Barron: "One of our early woman lawyers, who later became a judge of the Boston Municipal Court. . . . They had gone to school together. She was my mother's attorney for many years. . . . That may have had some influence too on my life and on my mother's attitude: that [Jenny Barron] was a successful woman lawyer."

After a successful time as a student at Girls High School, Gladys chose Portia Law School because it "was close to home and easy to get into. They didn't have any . . . entrance exams at that time. It was no effort. . . . It was practically around the corner from my home. . . . I didn't think [I] was so unique, but I thought the school was unique in that it was [only] for women."

Like other Portia students, Gladys remembered Bessie Page as "a [particularly] fine woman professor. . . . The school, of course . . . was more or less dominated by family. Dean MacLean and his wife taught there; . . . it was . . . a family affair." The MacLeans, however, underwent a divorce at about the time Gladys left school in 1936.

Gladys was "a little bit concerned" that Portia, unlike the university schools, was using the text and lecture method. "I felt [these other schools] might have done a little bit better with their students. Turned out better material. [But] the practice of law depends a great deal on the individual . . . regardless of what school you've gone to. [In] my later practice . . . I came in contact with lawyers who graduated from Harvard who absolutely were not as competent as some . . . who went to Suffolk. It was a question of how one adapted to practice. . . . I don't think the school mattered too much once you got into practice, because you've got to keep up your continuing education. . . . If you studied and you worked hard you could be as competent as anybody else who went to another law school."

One problem with Portia, however, was that though it had a debating club in which Gladys participated, "they didn't have moot court . . . which I think is one of the good things that the schools have now developed." Besides, the debating club was very peripheral as far as Portia was concerned. Thus, "I had a hard job when I went to court.

I had to prepare myself well before I tried a case on rules of evidence and that sort of thing; had I had that kind of training in law school, it would have come much easier.

"Many of the women who did graduate from law school—I'm not talking necessarily about Portia—did not go into active practice. A lot of them were afraid to do it. But I decided that I wasn't going to be tied down to any corner of somebody's office doing probate taxes [or] title work. . . . The majority of girls may have felt that they were being trained as helpmates, but there [was] a group of us . . . eager to be independent and practice on our own. . . . I didn't know exactly how I was going to start out in practice, but I hoped that I would be able to be a lawyer as such, and not be someone working . . . in a capacity that might be similar to a secretary in a law office."

There was also a group of students at Portia who "just took courses for the fun of it. Some of them just felt that they wanted to know something about law. They were married and had families. They were just doing this as a lark, more or less."

On the whole, very few of Gladys's class went into practice. Gladys, however, was fortunate. "It was through the liquor business that I [started] with clients. It would have been very difficult without that. . . . I got associated with an office through a hearing at the license commission.

"Before I passed the bar, my family had a package store. And people around were very professional and were looking for licenses near us. And it was customary to have a hearing at the licensing board when somebody applied." Gladys appeared before the board as a member of her family's corporation opposing the granting of an application to establish a store near them.

At the close of the hearing (in which the application was denied), the opposing counsel came over to Gladys's mother—an old friend—and said: "You've got a smart girl there."

"And my mother said, 'I'm waiting to hear from the bar.' I had taken the bar exam. He talked to me and said, 'You know, I'd like to have somebody like you in my office.' " Gladys responded that when and if she passed the bar she would come and talk to him.

"And I began to inquire about him, because I wanted to make sure that he was a reputable attorney. I found out that he was very well liked and was a very reputable man of good background. He had been practicing . . . for about 30–35 years. He was well established and well known. So immediately when I found out that I had passed . . . I went up to see him. And we made a very interesting arrangement. I was not to get any salary. Nobody got any salary in those days.

But I would have office space, in return for which I would do all his research. I had a free office, and I was able to turn to my own practice if necessary . . . but if he assisted me on anything we would split the fee." Gladys had not been hired as a glorified legal secretary.

"There was a secretary in the office, and I was aware of the fact that she would do the typing on my notes on my briefs . . . if I did any research. [Basically] I would prepare [not type] the lawyer's memorandums of law, briefs, and so forth for him. He seemed to have . . . a lot of confidence in me, which was very helpful. . . . I would prepare something and the day it would come to trial, he'd say to me, 'Well, you prepared it. You know more about it than I do. Now go try it.' He forced me into this business of trying [cases].

"It was really tough" [as a woman in court]. "You didn't know whether the judge wanted you to wear a hat, or not to put a hat on. . . . You didn't know exactly what the judge expected of you. There was one judge with the Boston Municipal Court . . . that was very, very gruff but he liked women. And whenever Mr. Levinson [the man she shared space with] had a case before [this judge], he would send me to try it. So I would do all right with it, because he liked the girls. But [usually] it was difficult, and you had this feeling when you had a lawyer on the other side, that [he] felt you were incompetent. . . . The other attorney . . . would say, 'What are you doing here? You don't belong.' They would take the attitude that you were totally incompetent and they were going to win the case hands down, because you knew nothing. Which was a decided advantage for me. . . . I never went into court without properly preparing a case. And I surprised them a little bit, because they didn't prepare their case. They figured they were up against somebody that knew nothing. And as a result of this I became fairly successful in litigation.

"I was with [Mr. Levinson] for a number of years because it was a very satisfactory relationship. And then when the war broke out, it was difficult getting offices so [the firm, which now had seven or eight lawyers] had to move. . . . We couldn't get exactly what we wanted . . . [and Gladys remained behind with a business broker who handled liquor licenses]. He wanted to give me a room in the office without any rent. . . . I anticipated that if I took that arrangement, I would be obligated to do all his legal work free. I said, 'Oh, no, I'll take the office, but I'll pay the rent.' So I did. I went in and we had a three-room suite and it was right next door to the [packagemen's] association office. So it was a very nice arrangement, and I stayed there for quite some time."

Despite this active professional life, Gladys Shapiro felt the family need to enter politics. Most of her clients were Italians, Albanians, and blacks, which gave her a broad base when coupled with her extensive ties in the Jewish community. She was a candidate for the Boston School Committee in 1945, running third in a year that two were elected. "It was the first time I ran for office and I didn't think about making out at all. I was the only woman that ran that particular time. And I got over 50,000 votes in the City of Boston.

"I had a lot of help from the Negroes, and I was active with the American Jewish Congress. Equal employment [legislation] was imminent—I was trying to get it passed, and I was active [in groups like] the Women's Trade Union. I lived in the West End, and the West End and North End were my ward. [The latter] was mainly Italian . . . so I had a lot of associations with people there. So I did have considerable help from the minorities, clients in a sense. Because of the showing I [made] in '45, I was induced to run in '47. There were three [elected] and I ran fourth."

The visibility helped her practice, and in retrospect she was not unhappy at losing, because "people were [always] looking for favors from school committeemen." Subsequently she ran in a primary for clerk of the Supreme Judicial Court and placed fourth out of sixteen candidates, carrying the City of Chelsea. Next she placed fourth in a race for Register of Probate of Suffolk County. Had affirmative action legislation been in place during this period, Gladys felt she "certainly would have some very important appointments," considering the governors she and her mother knew and the campaigns in which they had worked.

In Gladys's experience, World War II did not greatly expand opportunities for women lawyers in private practice "because a lot of them went into government work. They got jobs in agencies. In fact I was offered a position doing something in contract work for the Army, which I didn't do. I felt that I'd be better off staying in active practice" so as not to lose the clientele she was building. "I didn't want to take any job that was outside of my practice.

"There were openings . . . in particular agencies . . . that needed legal training. [Some of the women lawyers] stayed in those jobs. They got stuck into them, and they stayed there. They didn't come out of them. . . . I didn't see any measurable increase . . . in business because of the fact that men had gone to war. They were going and they were coming back. There were several in our suite that had gone into the service, and the older lawyers that didn't go in probably were getting that business instead of the women."

Gladys never allowed marriage to interfere with her busy career.

Other women lawyers who did marry only came back to practice "after a lapse of a great many years." Although her practice was never interrupted, Gladys still found the going hard because men "definitely discriminated" against her. "I have a little prejudice too. If I find a competent woman, I refer [cases outside of Gladys's specialty] to her." In this way, Gladys Shapiro engaged in a little informal women's networking.

The prejudice and discrimination Gladys faced made her question the role of an all-female law school. "I think it's important for you to have contact with men in law schools [because] you're going to be in contact with them in the practice.... I've always gotten along in the practice with men. And some of them have had a feeling at some time about women, but they've always considered me one of the boys. When I'm dealing with them in a situation, they respect me and consider me as one of them. I have no problem today, [but] I did have a lot of them [once].... We [at Portia] were not as well prepared [for discrimination] probably because...we were not harassed at school by men." A determined Gladys Shapiro, however, overcame this handicap to become a competent, trusted attorney, with "more men [clients] than women." Whether any woman ever fully became "one of the boys" is, however, questionable. In any event, this may have seemed an appropriate thing to say to this male interviewer.

Helene Lawrence: Dominant Personality in a Man's World

If personality forged a career for Gladys Shapiro in the face of the obstacles with which society confronted her, it may have been even a greater factor in the life of Helene Lawrence, class of '39.[22] A self-described "man's woman," this tall, commanding lawyer used her brains, ambition, and (in her own view) attractiveness, to take her a long way indeed.

Another protege of Bessie Page, Helene Lawrence married a Harvard man in her senior year and did little professionally for the first few years after passing the bar exam. Her husband, an investment counseler who had been attending Northeastern Law School at night, was commissioned in the Navy shortly after passing his bar exam. "After he left on an in-port training (San Francisco), I came back home and applied for a commission in the Navy, unknown to him, and was told I was not eligible because my husband was a commissioned officer." According to Helene, the Navy feared the possibility that she would rise in rank before he did.

"I didn't have any reaction at that time. It took me a while. I was brought up to be . . . a housewife, or a dental hygienist, or a nurse. And all of these concepts of what a woman should be in the '20's and '30's were innate, embedded in my vision. So I didn't—either I didn't know how to handle it, or I didn't recognize it, or if I recognized it, it didn't bother me. I accepted it. . . ." I [later] encountered [discrimination] several times. "In spite of [the fact] I didn't buck it, I did 'make it'. . . . If I had . . . conveyed the feeling that [she felt discriminated against], I wouldn't have made it.

"I realized as a woman attorney early on, that I'd have to prove myself to be not as big as the men, but better . . . and I never worked with anybody but men attorneys in my whole career with one exception." Her legal career started with the Coast Guard. "In training we were indoctrinated in military law, and military behavior. . . . I must say I hated every minute of it. At one point I wondered what I had gotten myself into. I could talk back to my husband, but I couldn't talk back to a superior officer.

"I think I was the first woman attorney . . . in the Coast Guard. I was assigned to doing military discipline research for infractions in the Merchant Marine, over which the Coast Guard has jurisdiction. [In reviewing one case, Helene] thought a particular [dirty] word the accused had used might have some significance. I didn't know what it meant. So I took it into the commanding officer and asked him to explain it. He said, 'I'll take that case, Mrs. Lawrence. You give that to me.' He didn't want to tell me what that meant. . . . [She eventually learned that it was] a sexual description by one male of another."

While in Washington, Helene also had the experience of being the prosecutor at what she believes to be the first all-female court martial in United States history. The defendants were female: "There were three women officers on the court . . . no man in the courtroom. . . . There was a plea of guilty. And [the accused] were given an undesirable discharge from the service. Now this [was] a double standard. Had they been men, they would have ended up in the jug. These two girls, who were deserters, were only charged with "Absent without leave." If they [had been] men they might have been charged with desertion. . . . They were charged . . . with a lesser offense and [given] an easy out."

Helene Lawrence and her husband were divorced just after the war in 1946. "I decided this time to launch myself all alone. I asked no alimony, and I decided to go under the GI Bill to . . . seek an elementary degree in French. . . . As soon as my divorce was granted, I went to Europe and did that. Before I went to Europe, I applied to the United States Navy Reserve [where she was commissioned] as a senior grade lieutenant. . . . The Navy wouldn't give me a legal classification. Why? Because I was a female. I was the only woman attorney in a class of about seventy male officers . . . anxious to keep up their reserve status." After studying French at the Sorbonne, Lieutenant Lawrence returned to Washington.

In November 1949, she received a telegram requesting her to report for duty at the Nuremberg military court. "Nuremberg is the end-of-the-world kind of job and I was the only woman attorney. . . . It was great. It was a law office, and I reviewed my first assignment. All trials by general court martial. These are serious trials. People can be in jail for the rest of their life. Serious criminal offenses, including murder, rape, incest. . . .

"At the same time I did that, I was a legal assistant. All the GIs on the post who had any legal problems would come to my office, be it taxes, divorces, child custody, alimony payments. I had a minor general practice for enlisted people overseas [with] home problems. And then I had all the reviews of the criminal courts martial to do. I was also assigned all over the command to teach military law." During this period, Helene Lawrence was the first American woman attorney ever to be admitted to practice before the High Commissioner of German Courts.

"Now from Nuremberg at the end of the wartime trials, I was promoted to attorney advisor to Seventh Army Headquarters in Stuttgart. I was a V.I.P. When the court made erroneous rulings of law . . . I would sift through these and comment on them to see whether they were effective for findings or sentence and dispose of them in one way or another. Then [I] later cut down the sentence. [I] had the authority to cut down the sentence if [I] thought it was too severe. That was an important job. It was a semi-judgeship. I was there five years and worked with two men in the review section.

"I had three judge advocates [as bosses] while I was there. The last one to arrive was a Colonel S. [name withheld]. There was a banquet to welcome him when he came. He was at the head of the banquet table . . . and I'm on his right, and he turned to me and said . . . 'Who are you?' I said, 'I'm Mrs. Lawrence, Colonel; I'm attorney advisor on your staff.' He said, 'What?' I said, 'I'm one of your attorney advisors, sir,' and he said, 'Well, you won't be very long if I have anything to do about it.'

"I was shocked, [but] didn't say anything. I batted my eyes at him and tried to be pleasant. The following morning at work I discovered that my desk had been removed from the legal department and set in the middle of 'chaos number 1,' all the enlisted men, sergeants, corporals and privates, where everybody came stomping in and out. Bedlam.

"I reviewed more general courts there than the whole time with the Army in Europe. I never once had a case returned to Washington for failure to recognize whether the law was incorrect or the verdict was in error, or not supported by evidence. Not one of my cases was ever "bounced" out of Washington. And none of the men [in my section were] privy to that honor."

Colonel S. broke his leg several months after moving Helene's desk. "I went up to the hospital to visit him, and I went into his room, and he looked at me and said, 'Are you coming here to see me?' I said, 'Certainly, Colonel. I was taught to visit the sick.' He said, 'I'll never forget this.' . . . He [also] realized I was doing more work than the men and better work than the men. . . . My desk was moved back up into the legal section.'

Nearing 40 years of age, Helene Lawrence decided to go home after five years in Germany. She wanted to get a legal job in the United States with the federal government before she got too old. "I came back, and then I had a rough time. Eventually, I was set with the Department of Justice. They had originally offered me a job in the law section, but I didn't want it, so I finally took a [lesser] job and ended up as a United States naturalization examiner with the Justice Department, in Washington, D.C., Los Angeles, and San Francisco." Helene had problems with her superiors in both Washington and Los Angeles, who wanted her to approve fraudulent depositions in the naturalization process. Thus she ended up in San Francisco doing "a famous [but top-secret] case" concerning the control of subversives.

"There were twelve men attorneys on the staff, and I was the only woman attorney. [There were] seven thousand pages of evidence [to read]. I held hearings sitting . . . on a raised dias; . . . I made the findings. This was a case that was pending in the Department of Justice. They had to get it off the books. It was subversive, really awful. . . . The Department sent a letter down the line [about] what a damn good job I had done—[how] painstaking."

Helene Lawrence retired because of cataracts in both eyes, wanting to leave "before my reputation went sliding." Her vision made it very difficult to operate in a courtroom. "If you're physically slowed down, you're mentally slowed down," she explained.

In Helene's view, this disability may have stopped her from achieving her final goal—a judgeship. Just before the illness struck, she had sent her qualifications to the Women's Bar Association in Washington.

This group, of which Helene was a long-time member, responded that they had reviewed her qualifications and at the first available appointment they were going to recommend her for a judgeship if she moved back to Washington. "I think if the eye problem hadn't occurred, I would have moved back to Washington, because I really wanted to sit on the bench."

Looking back at the law school that had prepared her for this active career, Helene Lawrence said of Portia that it had not been a hindrance to her to go to an all-women's school, but that the school's lack of national accreditation had been a handicap. "We felt like second-class citizens." Although Portia prepared her well, she had constant difficulties getting credit for her legal training once outside Massachusetts.

As for the "woman" issue, Helene Lawrence confronted it in the way that came most naturally to her. Since men "are the dominant force in society," Helene sought to make use of the fact that they "admire women who are feminine looking . . . particularly in the professions." Thus, Helene Lawrence tried to "get around" men like Colonel S. by "batting her eyes" at them, although her work seems to have been the crucial element in her success. Even more difficult to overcome than male attitudes may have been the fact that she had a degree from a law school accredited only in Massachusetts. She surmounted each of these obstacles through the force of personality and intellect, with little apparent help from other women.

*****

In analyzing the foregoing interviews, a clearer picture emerges of the world's only woman's law school. Since Portia took nearly everyone who applied, the educational experience was bound to be limited by the mediocre educational backgrounds of many of its students. Thus, the experience was particularly rough on exceptional students like Sarah Wallace. Yet, the school did provide access to the profession for self-starters with exceptional fortitude. Although it was run without the sense of mission that guided Washington College of Law, Portia provided legal training for large numbers of women who otherwise would not have had it. Thus, even without "pushing" its uniqueness, Portia Law School played a significant role in both the democratization of the bar and the professional advancement of women.

BOSTON UNIVERSITY WOMEN LAW GRADUATES

Grace Minton O'Hare: Woman in Law as Lawyer's Wife

Since Suffolk and Harvard took no women in the 1920's and 1930's (Suffolk admitted a few at the end of the 1930's), potential women lawyers in Boston had, besides Portia, only Boston University and Northeastern University to turn to. Boston College Law School, which began in 1929, took insignificant numbers of women. Since Northeastern had much the same socioeconomic mix as Portia and graduated very few women, one has to look to Boston University Law School for significant comparisons to Portia women.

Boston University Law School had begun admitting women in the late 1800's and generally had five, six, or more women per class in the 1920's and 1930's. Although BU, as might be expected with no Harvard for competition, enrolled a proportionately higher number of middle-class women than did Portia, significant numbers of their women had similar backgrounds. Still, BU required more education of its entrants, and this alone distinguished many of its students from Portia's.

Grace Minton began BU Law School in the fall of 1919, in the first class to enter after World War I.[23] Three hundred men flooded this class, and amidst them matriculated Grace and seven other women.

Grace had grown up in a solidly professional family in Jamaica Plain. Her father was a lawyer and Democratic state legislator; her mother, a Radcliffe graduate, taught third grade. They were second-generation children in the United States, their grandparents having emigrated from Ireland and England, respectively.

Grace's father, after leaving the legislature, had gone into private practice (largely probate) and then had been elected election commissioner for the City of Boston. Grace was only 14 when he died at the age of 45 years. After completing Girls' Latin School, she was accepted to Smith College, but, as the eldest of four children, elected to stay at home to help her mother with the family. Thus she attended BU Liberal Arts College for one disappointing year before entering law school.

Law school appealed to her immediately. She liked the seriousness of her male classmates. There was none of the emphasis on a "good time" that she had seen in college. Most of her classmates had only a high-school education; BU did not yet require college training for its law school.

Her women classmates were as serious as the men, but most did not anticipate future careers in the same sense as the men. Since women role models in law were few, women at the law school concentrated more on getting good grades than on entering a particular career path. Grace remembered the women as unaggressive on the whole, and traditionally "feminine." They treated slights about their sex with equanimity and did not push for change.

The BU women were from all kinds of backgrounds and types of schools; there were no striking reasons that they had chosen law. The father of one woman was a judge, but this was by no means typical of the others.

Grace remembered being treated "well" by her male classmates, many of whom, just "back from the war," were a lot older than the women. Her teachers, all men, treated her "well," too, though perhaps not so well by current standards. Any time a "sticky" part was reached in a course like domestic relations, the women were excused and left to read these chapters by themselves without benefit of lecture. In fact, it was quite common, whenever sex was to be discussed, for the women to be dismissed. Grace could not remember any of the women complaining about this treatment.

Grace contrasted this behavior with that which one might expect in similar circumstances today. "Girls today are a lot more aggressive than they were. . . . In my day they didn't rise up en masse and do something like they are doing today. Of course we had suffragettes—before my time."

Law school was a "hard course" for everyone. In contrast to those in the part-time law schools, Grace's B.U. classes met every weekday, beginning at 9 A.M. and sometimes lasting straight through until 3 P.M. Since BU had not yet switched to the case method of instruction (see Charlotte Slavit's story, which follows), Grace and the other students still studied in much the same way as the Portia students did. Usually they studied from texts written by professors and were intermittently quizzed on their comprehension.

Law teaching, despite the efforts of Harvard and the AALS, had not yet become a full-time profession. Most of Grace's teachers were very good lawyers with other jobs, who also taught law; Grace could remember only one who taught full-time. In some cases, a prominent visiting professor was brought in to teach. For example, former President Taft once taught a six-week course, leaving Grace with a bit of sage advice for any lawyer: never to fear telling a client that you don't know the answer to a question and that you will have to look it up.

After passing the bar exam, Grace had little chance to heed President Taft's advice for several years. Her job as an investigator with the Boston Finance Commission was primarily non-legal, but she did have the chance to write some briefs. After marrying her classmate John O'Hare, she began doing his probate work and family law. However, she raised her own family "quite early," a fact causing law to take a back seat.

"I happened to have some help in the house, so in that way, I was able to go out each day. It wasn't like a regular job. It was on my own time. And I found it easy." Grace was able to devote more time to practice once the children were in school.

In reflecting on her life in the law, Grace felt that the profession had been good to her. She didn't think that men had really discriminated against her in practice, but then "there wasn't anybody standing over me telling how wrong it was. . . . I 've been very fortunate. I've had a good marriage, a good career. Not outstanding, like some of the women later on that came along." Grace Minton O'Hare saw her career as falling into a generational gap between "the first pioneers like Judge Emma Schofield" and more modern successes. She accepted the reality that a married woman lawyer's career formed in the 1930's was likely to be episodic.

Charlotte Slavitt: A Lonely Path to Government Service

Boston University Law School moved quickly toward the Harvard model in the early 1920's. By the time Charlotte Slavitt entered BU in 1924,[24] the school required one year of college preparation for admission and was preparing to increase that requirement to two years in 1925. Charlotte was born in Fall River, Massachusetts, of parents who had emigrated from the Ukraine in 1880. Her father had been in his early twenties when he arrived in Massachusetts, and he and his wife already had several children. He went into the real estate business. Charlotte was the second-to-last of a family consisting of two boys and four girls. Her oldest brother stayed in real estate; her younger brother was a salesman. Two sisters were reasonably contented housewives. Another married twice and had a radio program in Chicago in the 1950's. Charlotte's older sister married several times and, when last Charlotte heard of her, had "run off" with her children.

In contrast to Jackie Guild's situation, Charlotte's decision to enter law school after one year of college precipitated a family crisis. Her father was firmly against her going to law school. Paradoxically, it was he who had generated her interest in the field. He was constantly talking about lawyers, and Charlotte decided that they must be very important. By the time she was 8 she had decided to become one of these important people, and she read about law and lawyers constantly during her years at Girls' Latin School.

Charlotte's father was blunt. "If you go to law school you'll become a lawyer and never get married." He thought this "unfeminine." Her mother, by contrast, though uninterested in "women's liberation" per se, saw nothing unusual in her daughter's desires. Charlotte—an independent, strong-willed individual—prevailed.

Unlike Portia's, BU's instruction was every day, full-time. This left little time for students to work to earn money; they had to have some family support. Also unlike Portia, BU by Charlotte's time used the case or "Socratic" method of instruction (copying Harvard). After all, BU was self-consciously a university law school, existing just as much in Harvard's shadow as Harvard existed in the shadow of the great European universities. Questioning students about great numbers of printed appellate court decisions was—Harvard had decided under Professor Christopher Columbus Langdell—the "academic" way of studying law. By Charlotte's time there was little lecturing by professors at BU about the rules of black-letter law. Here, unlike Portia, the students had to piece the "rules" of law together themselves.

Charlotte did not fare well under this "academic" mode of instruction. She recalls being "just about a minimum student." One professor who stood out in her mind was Felix Harper (pseudonym) whose subject was contracts and who, like Bessie Page, gave a successful private bar review course. In Charlotte's senior year, Harper began giving a bar course at Harvard, "which was a terrible disgrace for Harvard because they didn't think anybody could know anything more than what they learned in law school."

Being one of fifteen women in the entire law school evoked apparently contradictory responses from Charlotte. On the one hand, the men didn't "bother much" about her and the other women. However, "they might have felt you were a joke, or that you were there looking for a husband." In fact, none of the women that she could remember married any of their male classmates. In retrospect, at least, Charlotte was unaware of any overt antagonism, and felt "very comfortable." Though the boys may have gotten together and "pulled the girls apart" while shooting craps in the basement, she never knew about it. Yet, Charlotte admits "they didn't think you could read language," but it was "nothing you paid much attention to."

Charlotte's classmates, though most worked part-time, showed significant differences from Mildred's at Portia. Most came from cities outside Boston and only one had gone to Boston University for college. Charlotte remembers them as serious students who did their schoolwork. They, like she, felt like members of a privileged group of women "who since the first World War were given the chance to get out and do something for themselves in their occupation."

Charlotte recalled that most of her female classmates were Jewish (whereas Italians and Irish predominated at Portia); this concentration, if accurately recalled, may reflect the more solidly middle-class base of that ethnic group as opposed to the other two during the 1920's. This class difference also helps explain how the BU women could afford to go to college first and then to a full-time law school. Still, it does not explain the absence of WASP women at BU; the reason may be in different perceptions of the role of a woman's education in establishment families as compared with Jewish ones. Certainly, educated WASP women in Boston were not being trained in great numbers to become legal professionals. Without an urgent need to work to become part of the establishment, many taught for a while, and then married others of their social class.[25]

Charlotte herself was not significantly more financially secure than many of the Portia women. She had a half-tuition scholarship for her first two years and occasionally worked Saturdays in department stores and florist shops. She also had a part-time job in the registrar's office, recording attendance records. Still, the BU tuition was nearly four times higher than Portia's, and these piecemeal jobs and the half-scholarship for two years required some supplementation from home.

Despite the full-time nature of the education, Boston University Law School did not compel any particular feeling of "belonging" in Charlotte Slavitt. The facilities were primitive by today's standards, and there was only one legal sorority, which she did not join. Upon graduation, she worked in Felix Harper's law office until she could take the bar. After taking and passing it she moved to Chicago, where her sister lived: "I just didn't think there was that much opportunity in Boston for a woman."

Charlotte had a job with the Republican National Committee when she moved to Chicago in 1928. She was in charge of the young people just beginning to vote in Wisconsin. "I don't think we did very much for Herbert [Hoover, who was running against Al Smith].

"When I came back from the campaign, I began parading the streets looking for a job in a law office. Those damn cold winters . . . were terrible. Nobody needed a young woman, particularly one with no connections. I had no opportunity . . . of having any business, and certainly not in a foreign state, so to speak. I had no connections locally. And that was the beginning of the Depression.

"I opened a law office. That's all I could do. A tiny little place. And I began practicing by virtue of the kindness of judges. At that time they'd make appointments for criminal cases.

"I had saved a little money, and for the first few months I lived with my sister. At that time, there was no public defender.... And you were not paid by the state.... You got paid only if you could get the money out of your client. And this was the Depression..., and most of these people were up on criminal charges of one kind or another, and so it was a terrible struggle.

"I started [in criminal work] because that was the only way I could get both ... trial experience and clients. And gradually I just went in and took everything. In those years, you weren't that specialized. I had some anti-trust cases. I think I tried one of the first antitrust cases for a motion-picture producing company.... I had lots of divorce cases.... The problem was making a living, paying your rent and secretary, and paying [for] your apartment. And I was lucky in some ways because I got a lot of publicity on some of the [criminal] cases.

"Guards at the penitentiary and jail ... might be asked by people in the jail to recommend somebody, and occasionally they recommended me. But I gradually got out of that when Walter Winchell made a nasty crack about me. [This criminal law work] lasted until the Second World War, and then I came to Washington and the Attorney General's Office.

"I was there from '42 to '44 ... in the foreign agent's registration division. I had charge of the machinations and political operations of agents of foreign countries, both [government and private]. My specialty was the Balkan Countries—largely Yugoslavia and Czechoslovakia. So we had to deal with the leaders of government in exile.... When the Nazis moved into other countries, the government left and went to England ... and we had to deal with them because we were in large part responsible for what political activity was going on here on behalf of their expected return [after the war].

"I job-hunted during the war. I tried to get in the WACs [originally Women's Auxiliary]. Though Charlotte might have gotten into the WACs through political pressure, which she didn't use, a final complication arose. "I didn't pass the physical."

To Charlotte Slavitt, both the New Deal and the war were a "great opportunity" for women. "It was a great open door.... If you stayed at home you probably were able to get into law firms, because they were afraid the men would be drafted. If you went into government, there was the same opportunity there.... [Once in,] many [of the women] stayed.

"I'm not aware of any discrimination I faced in my practice, but ... you don't know how many people might have recommended you, only to be faced by the potential client saying, "Look, I don't want a woman lawyer." I was not aware of any discrimination on the part of judges [and] court personnel. Actually ... in Chicago at that time there were many women in [law]. They had three or four law schools which had admitted women. But there were not many women in [individual] practice at that time.... Some of them were with big real estate companies. [See the interview with Edna Cronin Smith (pseudonym) in the Chicago chapter]. Some [were with] banks. I think there were only three of us that were in practice individually, and not with a father, son, or relative—or husband."

There were several men who helped Charlotte Slavitt along. "There were judges who would send cases to me. Several lawyers who were very helpful." On the other hand, she had a very unpleasant encounter with a top male criminal lawyer, which occurred after just two or three years in practice. In the process of taking her first case to the Illinois Supreme Court, she was "bawled out" by this lawyer, when "all I did was ask him [for] a copy of his brief on a certain case. He told me I had no business trying to get into the Supreme Court with my lack of experience. And," Charlotte recalls, "he was quite right." On the other hand, how else could she gain the experience in a bar where no one had been willing to train her?

In government, Charlotte remembered more "inchoate discrimination" than in private practice. "Many of the lawyers in that era had gone into government when they couldn't cope outside." They would tell Charlotte she didn't have "to support a wife and children," and be very competitive with her for promotions. "And you [had] a kind of hierarchy set up, where you can only have so many stenographers and so many lawyers at this level and so many at the other, so it's quite a scramble for those men....

"Promotions were a matter of who your boss was.... Lawyers were in a so-called excepted position under civil service. They were not part of the civil service routine, although they had the same privileges. Because of the less rigid routine it was more open for personal prejudices on the part of the bosses.... They would rather deal with a man ... because they were not used to dealing with women [as lawyers], as young men are now.... They could more easily go to lunch [with men]. They could play golf with them. There was a lot of that in that kind of situation."

Charlotte felt that she was "very lucky. I had some very able bosses. I can't honestly say I had any real problems. Certainly none of the discrimination." However, having worked for the Corps of Engineers for a time, Charlotte saw a real problem with less competent bosses in the military. "The mere fact that a man moves from Desk A to Desk B" meant, the military thought, that "he was imbued with all the knowledge that he needed to be boss of that desk. You had to educate your boss. So that was a problem."

A short venture in post-war Washington—starting a company to sell surplus war equipment—failed for Charlotte. "That was a riotous time. . . . Every congressman's office, every senator's office, every one who'd ever been in government was in the racket." Charlotte spent the rest of her career hopping from agency to agency in the federal government. These included Labor, Defense, and the Navy.

Charlotte Slavitt had become a lawyer the hard way. Seeing a lack of opportunity in her native Boston, she had made her career in "foreign" cities, Chicago and Washington, a woman without connections. Her credo was to get "all [the training] you can, while you can, where you can. And then if you have a rich husband or a rich father or a good uncle in a big law firm, by all means, don't be an ass. Go in there and get the job." The "good uncle" never existed for Charlotte Slavitt; she went it alone and unafraid, apparently without the help of other women. She often had to rely on men, both for her criminal cases and her promotions in government.

*****

The stories of Grace Minton and Charlotte Slavitt suggest several things. First, they were women of more solidly middle-class origins than many Portia women. They were somewhat better educated, and both psychologically and physically more mobile. Despite the slights of male teachers and students, both appear to have been able to cope with much of the harassment at school. Still, there was little sense of solidarity with the other women; each saw herself more as an individual, putting up with the awkwardness in being in a tiny minority because this was the best way to reach her personal goals.

Surely, BU women were by graduation more attuned to how the male-dominated bar would treat them than were the Portia women. For example, Charlotte's quick decision to move to Chicago showed an appreciation of what she would face in the Boston bar. These were realistic, "no-nonsense" women, better equipped by nature and opportunity than most Portia women to face the reality of being female lawyers ahead of their time.

The careers of O'Hare, Slavitt, and their female classmates were generally more "successful" than those of Portia women. For instance, Portia graduates of the period included no full-time jurists. Meanwhile, the 150 or so women graduates of BU during the 1920's and 1930's produced several jurists, including the locally prominent Emma Fall Schofield, who occasionally taught part-time at both BU and Portia. In various ways they were a more select group than the Portia women; though their stories do not reveal the success that men of similar background and ability enjoyed, they made substantial professional inroads for a small group, both in Boston and elsewhere.

4

Washington: Big Government and the Beginning of Networking

A MORE OPEN, POLITICAL BAR

If Boston was a center of European immigration, Washington, the gleaming Federal City on the Potomac, was Mecca for many native-born Americans. While power in Boston was centered in higher education and corporate finance, Washingtonians were engaged in the business of government. The fact that law in the District of Columbia was dominated by the federal government, rather than by the Harvard-State Street combine as in Boston, led to marked differences in the legal education of women in the two cities.

All law schools in Washington, even those like Georgetown and

George Washington, which had national ambitions, had evening or part-time divisions. In large part this was because the schools had a primary role as a stepping stone for those employed in government service. In some sense, these were *all* working people's schools, and their faculty, administrators, and students were all involved in some way in the practical business of running a nation. The leading politician, rather than the great scholar, was the model for the legal education provided in Washington schools.

Still, there was a hierarchy among the law schools, with Georgetown and George Washington at the top, and Catholic and Washington College of Law at the bottom. The cleavage between a Georgetown and a Washington College of Law, however, was not as sharp as between a Harvard and a Suffolk or Portia. The similarity of mission of the Washington schools and the similarity of their student bodies rendered the distinctions less sharp, causing none of the acrimony that existed, for example, between the Harvard of Dean Pound and the Suffolk of Dean Archer. Thus, the movements of Washington College of Law from a textbook method of instruction, centering on preparation for the local bar, to the casebook method, and from local to national accreditation, were much smoother and quicker than Portia's.

Founded by feminists, WCL was a haven for a number of women in the national women's movement, including those like Alice Paul '22, founder of the National Women's Party and author of the Equal Rights Amendment,[1] and her assistant, Sue White, who had helped win women's suffrage in 1920.[2] A number of women WCL graduates throughout the 1920's and 1930's shared the sense of mission of its founders Emma Gillette and Ellen Mussey. The federal government provided them with employment, the city with a national forum, and WCL with the training necessary for effective action.

Even in the early 1920's, then, WCL was not primarily the school of the Alice Pauls and Sue Whites. For example, the progressive Emily Harris of Massachusetts, who became dean in 1924, was forced to leave after an unsuccessful one-year struggle to put the school on a more full-time basis. She had been educated first at Portia, where her father, U.S. Representative and Massachusetts Probate Judge Robert O. Harris, was chairman of the board. Apparently, the low-profile patriarchy of Arthur MacLean did not suit her, and she enrolled at WCL in the woman's suffrage period during World War I. When she was appointed dean, Harris was amazed to see her school taking a Portia-like stance. She failed to get tuition and entrance requirements raised, and thus to hire a full-time faculty. Instead the board kept tuition low and faculty participation episodic in recognition of the primary interests of students and faculty in other work, usually with the federal government.[3]

What feminists at WCL and elsewhere in Washington faced was well exemplified in Sue White's 1931 newspaper debate with Dr. Nolan Lewis, a psychiatrist at St. Elizabeth's Hospital in Washington, entitled "Should a Woman be President of the U.S.?"[4] The "debate" began with Miss White stating her position:

> Women can be long-suffering, many of them can act with decision, and fight, without bloodshed or the use of physical force, in a rather deadly way. These attitudes of patience, combined in one exceptional, intelligent, able individual would lend a much-to-be-desired dignity to the role of Chief Executive.
>
> Nervous worrying, ineffectual muddling and petulance do not make a good President, male or female, but obviously these are not exclusively feminine traits, nor are they common to all, and in discussing Presidents are not to be charged against the hypothetical female any more than against some of the real 'old-womanish' gentlemen who may have aspired to the exalted position. Unstatesmanlike qualities cannot always be avoided in a woman President. ... But we are now imagining ... a highly evolved human being, an exceptional individual. ... Should she be admitted to her destiny, wherever it may lead her, in this land of equal opportunity? I say yes. What say you?

Dr. Lewis, of course, said no—and the message was blunt, even in this city of women lawyers' greatest opportunity. Although he agreed with Sue White that man had contradicted himself over and over again in his efforts to define the relationship between himself and woman, Dr. Lewis's reason was striking: "[F]ew investigators will deny that the chief [reason for this] is the contradictory emotional behavior of the woman herself in times of stress, an attitude which is more outstanding than in men and which would not inspire confidence in a chief executive. . . ."

As for hereditary queens who had interrupted the "usual male line of rulers, . . . anyone interested to learn may convince themselves of the almost complete dependency of these rulers in their male advisors and chief executives.

"I agree that a woman should be 'admitted to her destiny' whatever that may be and however it may be interpreted, but I am convinced by the psychological reasons set forth . . . that there is no sign at present for that 'destiny' to be centered in the presidential chair, an opinion which is reinforced when 19 of any 20 men and 18 of any

20 women consider the question as premature, as absurd, or as a joke when approached on the subject."

Confronted with snide sentiments like these from even highly "educated" men like Dr. Lewis, most WCL graduates were even less forthright than Sue White. The overriding impression is certainly not one of radicalism. In addition, it has often been observed that Washington is really a southern city; its women share a southern tradition of gentility, which is genuinely conservative, although occasionally fueled by a quiet activism. With suffrage a reality, most Washington women in law pursued both individual and group goals from a position decidedly in the mainstream. Even in the New Deal, this often meant taking clerical or secretarial positions in government. No women were examined at all for the professional grades of associate, junior, or senior attorney in 1930 or 1938. Only in one year during the New Deal—1935—do the figures show women in government getting professional rank as lawyers.[5]

Still, many women law graduates found work with the federal government, if not usually of professional grade. They were aided in this task by a small, but relatively effective, informal network of female government attorneys. These women lawyers, because of their central location and employment opportunities, comprised perhaps the most successful network of women lawyers anywhere in the 1930's. They also belonged to formal networking organizations such as the Women's Bar Association of D.C., Women Lawyers Association, and the Kappa Beta Pi legal sorority.

These women included Anne Agnes O'Neill, WCL Class of 1911, assistant to the legal advisor of the State Department;[6] Rebecca Greathouse, WCL Class of 1925, assistant U.S. attorney and secretary of the National Women's Party;[7] Burnita Shelton Matthews, practicing attorney, officer of the Women Lawyers Association with Ellen Spencer Mussey, and instructor in evidence at WCL;[8] and assistant attorneys general Annette Adams, Helen Carloss, and Mabel Walker Willebrandt.[9]

When another member of the network, Annabel Matthews, WCL '21, was appointed to the U.S. Board of Tax Appeals in 1930, she came under heavy pressure from Mabel Willebrandt to hire female assistants. Matthews's papers reveal the network in action as the new commissioner responded to job requests from males of her home state of Georgia.

A June 2, 1930 letter from Matthews to Ralph R. Quillian of Atlanta was right to the point: "I have not yet appointed my second legal assistant, but I expect to select a woman lawyer. In view of this fact, I suggest that you do not apply for the position." On June 25, she sent a somewhat nicer letter, saying the same thing, to a Bertram Boley of Atlanta. He refused to be deterred, responding that "this is not a matter of gender, but experience. Employ me for a year or two until you find a suitable attorney." This letter, however, met with Ms. Matthews's straight-forward response of June 8: "I have to advise that I have secured a woman attorney whom I wanted as an Assistant, and there is, therefore, no occasion for giving your application further consideration."[10]

Needless to say, few women lawyers of the 1920's and 1930's had the power to make the choices that Annabel Matthews could. Fewer still were willing or able to surmount the professional concerns of their position to make affirmative action for other women their paramount concern.

WCL AND GEORGE WASHINGTON UNIVERSITY STUDENTS

Maude Rollins Pryse: An Alternate Career Path

Mrs. Maude Pryse, in 1982 (at age 88) a member of the National Board of the Muscular Dystrophy Foundation, entered the still-unassuming WCL in 1927.[11] A native of Baltimore, she lived in several residential areas of that city and lost her father, a teamster, when she was but 12 years old. In her interview, she remembered in detail that during the great Baltimore fire of 1904 her father didn't come home for three days: "He had to stay with his horses [which pulled his wagon], and move them from place to place."

Unlike her father, Maude's mother, who was faced with the task of raising all six children upon his death, had had several years of high-school education. All six children got good educations, including a sister who became a doctor and a brother who became a "very mighty attorney in Baltimore." Maude was proud of the line of Virginians on her father's side, especially of her grandfather, Colonel Rollins, who was killed with Moseby's Raiders in the Civil War. "I was very determined that his [grandchildren] were going to have a good education." Rollins's wife, whom he had married when she was 13 years old, had a busy life raising their thirteen children, including Maude's father, who picked up shipments from the steamers that plied the Potomac, bringing produce to market from the farmers who tilled its shores.

Her mother's mother came from the "very noted Lindsay family" and had married a contractor. Both families were Scottish and English and some members had come to America before the revolution. Maude had traced her mother's side back to Benjamin Bradford of Virginia, and through him to the Allens, Withers, and Keyes in Britain in 1541.

Maude's mother went to work in a factory to support her brood. Maude herself began work at 12 while attending school at night. After finishing high school, she took shorthand and typewriting and English at the Baltimore City College Evening High School, and worked as a stenographer. During the war year of 1917 she worked at Hooper Wood Mills as secretary to its president; this corporation was busy "making tents and things like that for the army."

Maude married in 1924. A graduate of Oregon State University, her husband had gone to school at the University of Wisconsin and in France where he enlisted as a private in the war and came out as lieutenant. "His fetish was education, as was mine." They married when Maude was 29 years old.

In 1927, after Mr. Pryse had graduated from law school at George Washington and had taken the bar exam, Maude became pregnant just as her husband was going away on an extended inspection trip for the Indian Forest Service of the Indian Bureau. She was working at the old-line (1796) real estate firm of Storey and Company and decided to attend WCL at night. This was the fulfillment of an old ambition of Maude's, stemming from her brother's example. She didn't talk it over with her brother; she just went.

After the first semester was over and Maude had gained high marks, she decided, though her husband was back and her pregnancy more advanced, to continue in school. "I went on to the next semester and got to within seventeen days of the birth of my [only] daughter."

Maude entered WCL because "George Washington University had gotten to the point where they couldn't accept anybody unless they had a college degree." WCL was accepting people who had the equivalent of a college education, and her business experience sufficed. Though serving as an example, Maude's brother was no help on the personal side. "He might have said, 'Oh, well, what do you want to fool with that for?—get married,' you know. That's what so many of them used to say."

While in school, Maude was particularly impressed by Professor Ed Mooers, who taught her contracts, criminal law and procedure, and real estate. "He was probably the finest law teacher that anybody ever listened to. I never saw . . . anybody who could teach law and make you understand like Ed Mooers. He lectured and to get his points across he used examples." Maude and several men in the class were favorite targets for questioning on these examples. "If anybody could not have understood that particular case the way he put it forth, then they were absolutely ignorant."

She remembers Mooers as "so brilliant and so knowledgeable. I really worshipped at the man's feet because he was just so good up against the rest of the professors. Really there was no comparison. . . . Anybody who was ever in my class would say the same thing. He expected [us] to be top-notch."

The books Mooers and others used consisted partly of cases and partly of explanations. "But then you also had to do your research" on certain problems and hand in assignments. Quizzes and examinations complemented the rest of the work. "You didn't loaf in [Ed Mooers's] class."

There was no loafing at home either, in Maude's first year at school. She would race home after her 9-to-5 job to her apartment in downtown Washington. After her husband returned from his long inspection trip, he helped to fix dinner every night, "wash dishes and take care of everything." Then, "I would race off to school."

During the second year of school, Maude did not work, remaining home during the day to take care of the baby, Brenda. At the end of the day, "I would put her in the back of the car and go downtown with her. My husband would meet us after work and take her home and take care of her [while] I went to school." The new regime continued through the end of school, with Maude attending the 5 P.M. session of classes rather the later one.

As she progressed through her years at school, she remembered classes being held first on the second, and later on the first, floor of the law school. The second floor consisted of an office at the top of the stairs, in back of that a medium-sized classroom, and finally the library. The first floor consisted chiefly of a large classroom, which had in front of it a small "gathering place." The school was "really very small. It wasn't a large number of students. . . . It was not what you have now by any means." (In fact, with the small day class initiated in 1929, the school ran three daily sessions, accommodating more students *in toto* than Maude may have imagined.)

Maude, with a cooperative husband gainfully employed, finished law school during the early evening session and did not go back to work or take the bar until an incident sparked her to in 1934.

In that year, Maude and Brenda were on a trip with Mr. Pryse in New Mexico. "We were visiting someone who said 'Brenda, what do you want to be when you grow up?' 'I want to be a lawyer. My daddy's a lawyer and my mother's a half-lawyer.'" Maude, shocked out of complacency by her 6-year-old daughter, asked Brenda why she had called her mother a half-lawyer. "Well, you've never taken the bar." Later in a private conversation with her husband, Maude mentioned the incident as "a cute thing to say." Mr. Pryse responded, "Well, she's right."

When the family returned to Washington, Maude enrolled in a popular bar review course, taking the exam in December 1934. "My husband would take me down [to the exam] in the mornings and pick me up at night. The first day was very good." The night before, Maude had gone to bed and dreamed about a doctrine of law, "the doctrine of something-or-other, I've forgotten now what it was, and I dreamed I had gotten that question and I didn't know the answer and I awoke and got out of bed and went into our library and got the book down." My husband asked me what I was doing, and I told him I was looking up the answer to the question in my dream. And he said, 'Come on back here to bed, and get back to sleep.' But I found the answer. You can believe this or not, [but] that was the second question on the examination. To use an expression, [the first day] was a humdinger.

"The second day I came out and said, 'I am not going back tomorrow. It makes no sense . . . to go back. . . . I know I failed.' My husband responded that if I didn't go back I would never know. 'You're not going to give up. You've never failed anything and you're not going to fail now." So I went back the third day [and it] wasn't bad."

In contrast to the Massachusetts bar exam, the D.C. exam contained no oral or discretionary component. Thus, the gruelling three-day experience was all that Maude needed to become a "full lawyer," and by passing it, she became one. Like her husband, who was an engineer using his law degree in his contracting, she did not practice law, except occasionally. She remained a real estate salesman with an established firm, taking probate cases on the side from time to time. Although she got a civil service appointment as a lawyer in the late 1930's, she didn't take it, valuing the freedom that her flexible schedule allowed. This freedom was enhanced by the domestic help which two careers could pay for. All in all, Maude's adaptation to the problems of being a woman in law seem sensible and rewarding. She used her training in a related field, lived a comfortable life, and found time for charitable activities with the Muscular Dystrophy Foundation.

Janet Morgan: A Lawyer on Her Own

In contrast to Mrs. Pryse and many other WCL graduates, Janet Morgan (pseudonym), who attended in the 1930's, became a practicing lawyer.[12] Born in North Carolina on a farm near Greenville, she lived there until her family moved to Virginia, where she has lived ever since. After high school, she attended Strayer's Business College in Washington and then took a position as secretary in a Fairfax, Virginia, law firm.

Janet's mother had graduated from Chowan County College in North Carolina. Her career was raising five children. Janet's father was a farmer both in North Carolina and Virginia. Her oldest brother was in the electrical and air-conditioning business in Florida. The next brother started as a teller in the Vienna Trust Company (now the United Virginia Bank in Vienna, Virginia) and rose to become its president and chairman of the board. Her only sister married and became a housewife. The youngest brother was in the Navy, and upon his retirement worked on naval affairs for the Department of Transportation.

Janet's father died when she was ten years old. "My mother didn't particularly have any plans for me. When I graduated from high school, I really did not know what I wanted to do, but I knew some things I did not want to do. I did not want to teach school. I was given an opportunity to live with an uncle and his family and to go to college and learn to be a teacher. I did not want to do this. [But] I knew that it was necessary for me to secure a position, work, and contribute to the support of the family and the education of my younger brother and sister.

"I was working at a law office. I liked law very much indeed. By the time I went to law school I was doing considerable work in the office, examining titles, drawing . . . wills and contracts. . . . I decided one day that I liked law well enough to go to law school and become a lawyer, rather than just being a secretary and title examiner."

Janet's mother had no particular influence on the decision to study law, and the man she worked with discouraged it. "He didn't like women studying law. And . . . he had a son who was going to graduate from law school. He did not see a place in the office for his son and also for me. . . . I had been working about eight or nine years before I considered going to law school, because of the financial situation. Salaries at this time . . . were very, very low. You worked six days a week and the pay was very little. I had a mother and a younger brother and younger sister to support.

"I must say, the first year was really very hard. There was very little time to study, and I think I went back the second year just to prove I could do it. In that year I had gotten into learning how to study and becoming used to studying. And it was much easier. . . . I had some encouragement from the Dean [of WCL]. As I said, the funds were very limited and she would let me finish one spring, [and not pay] my tuition until I was back in the fall. Each time she let me continue school."

Janet had other encouragement as well: "The daughter of the treasurer of Fairfax County offered to pay my expenses in law and to advance me the money, and I of course would repay her. . . . I think that encouraged me to go, even though I didn't borrow the money from her [because she didn't think she would make enough money to repay the woman]. Then I had one more friend who assisted me in whatever way she could, encouraged me to go, and when things looked a little bit bleak she would encourage me to hang in and keep going.

"I would say when I finished law school that I was much further ahead than the other students. Many of [them] worked for the government. I had worked in a law office and was working in a law office at the time I was in school. When I finished, I felt I was head and shoulders ahead of them, because not only did I know how, but I knew why."

Since she didn't meet the educational requirements for the Virginia bar, Janet took the D.C. bar exam before graduating, failing it the first time. Before "taking the bar the next time . . . I went to Washington and managed an office building, [finished law school,] and took . . . a cram course. . . . The District bar, you know, lasts three days, and it's really quite hard. You compete with people from Harvard and Yale, perhaps, and they all want to come down and get jobs with the government. And this time I was working for a Frenchman [a Mr. Montague], who was really very, very kind to me. He owned the office building. He said that I could take two weeks off to study for the bar and if I passed, fine. If I did not, I could take a month, two months, so I really got encouragement from this man."

This time Janet passed the bar exam and "hung out her shingle" at Mr. Montague's office building, which she managed. "The Frenchman let me practice and where I got my clients, I do not know, but I did. And of course there were . . . some very good firms in the building." Edward L. Burroughs, one of Janet's teachers at WCL, was located there in the firm of former Attorney General Cummings, which sent her business.

Like Edwin Mooers, Burroughs had been one of Janet's favorite teachers at WCL. He and the others "worked on me a little bit harder because I was shy. They probably asked me more questions, and I think they were doing that on purpose to get me to stand up and recite." Of the women professors, Janet could remember only Dean Riley well. "I had two or three other women professors, but I don't recall their names. The men impressed me more."

Evidently, Janet Morgan had impressed Professor Burroughs while at school, and she further impressed him and his partners in her first year practicing law. "Another man in the firm . . . was very instrumental in helping me. He used to teach at the University of Virginia." With this assistance, Janet Morgan's practice got going, and she eventually achieved her dream of practicing in Fairfax, where she works to this day.

Elizabeth Salisbury Denny: Sorority and Government as an Extension of Family

The federal government, however, provided the chief avenue of access for Washington women in law. Elizabeth Salisbury Denny, WCL '35, became a naval officer and eventually an important figure in the selective service system under General Lewis Hershey.[13] Her story, provides a picture of what bright, active women lawyers in Washington were able to achieve with maximum effort.

Elizabeth was born in Washington, D.C., on 9th Street, N.E., just nine blocks from the Capitol. In 1917, when she was 5 years old, her father, who came from a very rural community and did not want to raise his children in the city, moved to Davisburg, Maryland, "which at the time was comparable to the moon. Once a month we would crank up the model T Ford and go to visit our grandmother and grandfather who still lived on 9th St., N.E. . . . In 1920 my father found out that there was some property available in Virginia at a very reasonable price in the middle of a five-hundred-acre woods, so he bought two acres where Moseby's Raiders used to hide after the Civil War.

"Not only did we have the big woods, but we had a brook down the bottom of the hill, and so our city cousins were always harassing their parents to bring them out to visit the Salisburys, and we'd all take our shoes off and go wading and pick flowers in the woods, and they thought that was a great deal. We always thought it was a great deal to go to Washington to visit our city cousins because then we could go roller skating. You can't roller skate on dirt roads too well.

"In 1920 papa's father and brother came down from Connecticut and helped him build this twelve-room house which we lived in. Not only did we have the big woods and lots of cool air and space, but we had a school, all seven grades in one room. [It was] taught by an old-time school teacher. . . . When I was in the fifth grade there were five boys and me . . . and I could play baseball with a hardball—I could outrun the boys . . . . I had two brothers younger than me by that time. I eventually had three brothers younger than me and three sisters younger, and I was the second mother for many of those years because my mother was busy having the children, and not enjoying the best health. . . . When I was in the fifth grade the old lady schoolteacher retired and they brought in a youngster, age 21, and we did have some little bratty kids. [The new teacher was doing well to] maintain discipline, much less teach anything, [so my mother] decided that was not for [her children]."

Since Elizabeth's father worked for the government, she could go to a Washington, D.C., school without paying tuition. In 1925, her parents arranged for the children to come to the city to school. Elizabeth became enrolled in a school at 9th and D, near her aunt's home. "I went there one year. Then . . . I went to junior high school at Thomas Jefferson High . . . which was at 6th and D, S.E. . . . . We had a trolley running out to Virginia and you could get to town in half an hour or less.

"So we rode the trolley . . . with a whole bunch of school kids . . . which was an education. They had a motorman and a conductor on those trolleys, which was a good thing because the conductor could maintain discipline while the motorman was running the car. . . . Those were the days when the black people had to sit in the back of the trolley. We kids thought there must be something nice about the back of the trolley. So whenever we thought we could get by with it, we'd sit in the back. . . . One time the conductor was coming along, and he said, 'Now you kids move up front there. You wouldn't want the black people sitting in your part of the trolley.' So we moved up where we belonged. And of course, the schools everywhere were segregated.

"My first career conference [in the seventh grade], I still recall very clearly. At this point I was 13 years old maybe, and we already had seven children behind me, some of whom didn't live, and when it came my turn I said I was going to be a mother. [The] little boys in the class, after the class was over . . . gave me an awful ribbing. I think I was the only one in the class that was going to be a mother. Every one else had been in the school system long enough that you could do something else, and they said, 'Elizabeth, are you going to bother to get married, or are you just going to be a mother?' So I decided maybe I'd better bury that ambition."

Elizabeth's father was from Connecticut and did not have a high school education. His own father had been a carpenter and/or blacksmith and had no money with which to educate him further. "In 1909 my father had decided to take the government exam for stenographer, and come to Washington and work for a year; . . . live in a boarding-house and save his money" and to then go back to Connecticut, where "he and his father would raise poultry." While in Washington Mr. Salisbury spent his "off-time researching his family tree . . . and started singing in the church choir at the 9th Street Christian Church at the corner where my mother lived. My mother was the lead soprano and pretty soon the chicken project fell by the wayside." The soprano who was to become Elizabeth's mother was descended from two large Scottish-Irish families of modest distinction; in fact, her father had been born and raised in Ireland, where he had been a schoolteacher and farmer.

Serving as a clerk in the Bureau of Naturalization of the Labor Department, Mr. Salisbury married Elizabeth's mother and never went back to Connecticut. "He did go to night school . . . to take some general education courses to make up for his lack of high school training. He also . . . studied drafting . . . and did a lot of painting and built [that] twelve-room house. Pop [had gotten] as far as he could go in the government [without] a law degree" by the late 1920's.

Illness in the Salisbury family caused Elizabeth to leave school for six weeks in 1928 to take care of 1-year-old twins for her mother. She was in no hurry to get married. "By the time I was 18 I knew what it was to have babies. If you [got] married, you had babies, you scrubbed the floors, you cooked meals.

"Mama was an avid crossword puzzle worker. She could outspell her kids upside down and crossways. She had a brilliant mind. But her mother had ten children and her ambition was to have ten children . . . [T]hat was my early ambition, but I got over it. She was . . . a marvelous mother."

By the time she graduated from high school in 1929, the automobile had become dependable enough as a means of transportation that Mr. Salisbury drove the three children who were in city schools in with him to work. The children got out at 3:30 and waited till Mr. Salisbury finished work at 4:30 in order to catch the ride back to Virginia. Elizabeth's father was "anxiously waiting" for her to finish high school so that he could go to law school. There was a promotion coming up in San Francisco that required a law degree—it would be a substantial promotion for him and he wanted to try it. "When I graduated, he could have gotten me a job anyplace, but I had a very, very dear friend who lived . . . where we lived, who had gone to Strayer's Business College [for the secretarial course], and [who] ended up as the private secretary to the president of George Washington University. I thought that would be the ultimate. So [a] major ambition was to be a private secretary to a big-shot. I didn't ever expect to have any glory of my own.

"So I out-talked my father and persuaded him to let me go to Strayer's Business College." Her father told her that if she got a job correcting papers, as her friend had, in order to pay for tuition, he would feed, clothe, and furnish transportation to her for another year. Elizabeth got the job and graduated in June 1930. "The guarantee of the school [was] that if you finished their secretarial course they would get you a job. Well, in June of 1930, there weren't many jobs."

Eventually she landed a job operating a mimeograph machine for the George Washington Bicentennial Commission, celebrating the 200th anniversary of Washington's birth. "A young man working at the bicentennial commission took my fancy and promised me the moon, the stars, and a whole lot of other things. . . . Here I was making plans for wedding bells, and he wasn't planning anything like that at all. [When this] finally dawned on me . . . I went into what would be called a deep depression." During this period, Elizabeth had an important discussion with her father, who, pursuing his promotion, had entered Washington College of Law evening classes in 1930. "He'd been bugging me to go to law school—Would I try it for one semester? If I didn't like it then he wouldn't say anything more. 'You have too fine a mind to waste the rest of your life being a mimeograph operator.' Tuition was reasonable. During the Depression they let you go to school on credit. I went on credit the whole first year." This was also the third and final year for Mr. Salisbury, who had been admitted as a special student because he had no high school, but was having little trouble with his studies.

Elizabeth's mother did not push in the opposite direction. "No, my mother was very wary of this mopey daughter. [Also] she [had begun] to see that having ten children wasn't necessarily the ultimate ambition in the world." During school, Elizabeth continued to work as a mimeograph operator, but upon graduation in 1935 she was able to get a stenographic job with the Treasury. As she had told her father continually, "Who ever heard of a woman lawyer?"

Elizabeth was quickly made aware of the feminist tradition of WCL when she entered the school. "How do you think I got all this women's lib stuff in the 1930's. . . . I joined the Kappa Beta Pi legal sorority [which] was very proud of the fact that they had as their honorary members Miss Mussey, who had founded the school, and Miss Gillette, who was the co-founder. [Grace] Riley . . . was then the dean of the school. We had women law school deans until this John [Sherman Myers] came along in the 1940's."

This tradition, however, was not what made Elizabeth feel comfortable at WCL. "I felt . . . comfortable at WCL because my father was going there . . . because the tuition was reasonable [and] because they let me go on credit for a whole year. The only reason I knew I had passed my courses [after a semester] was because the sorority rushed me and they didn't rush you unless you had an 85 percent average. At the end of the first semester [under her agreement with her father], I had to keep going until I could find out what grades I had made."

The main reasons Elizabeth went to and stayed in law school seemed to be her father's persistence and the school's location, conveniently close to both her office and her father's. Kappa seemed influential as well. "My first social activities of any kind were in law school. [The women of Kappa Beta Pi] were all very successful. One of them had grown up around the corner from my mother, which gave me an entree, and later [she became a trustee] of WCL. [Also there was] an officer in one of the local banks [named] Helena Reed. Another member was a woman who worked in my father's office [who] knew me from [the time I was] a little girl. . . . [It was like] an extended family, and something I had never really experienced." Elizabeth's affinity for Kappa was so great, she has continued as its historian to this day.

"[The sorority] took you in and made you feel like you were really somebody, and elected you to office. You went to dinners in a long formal gown, on the Shoreham Terrace, and there were all kinds of things. It was interesting. Of course, we'd always have meetings, and nearly always would have somebody talk about what they were doing in the legal field. I had a number of friends who were secretaries. As soon as they got out of law school they were going to get themselves a legal job. I was a mimeograph operator. As soon as I got out of law school, I was going to get a secretarial job. I wasn't expecting anything great."

Elizabeth's routine was typical of her classmates. Every weekday afternoon at 4:30 she left work on the mimeograph machine at the WPA and walked a few blocks to WCL, where class met from 5 to 7. Then she went home with her father to eat the second of the two dinners her mother would cook: "one for the kids who were in school and one for papa and me." The method of instruction at WCL was largely text, not case: "It was sort of like high school. All you had to do was learn what they had in the assignment." This rote learning was supplemented by quizzes, moot court, and debating, and by the case method in one class—constitutional law. However, even when using a text, the professors would call on students during their lectures.

Elizabeth was largely unaware that other, "better" law schools were using the case method. "The only thing I knew about other law schools were the ones that had Kappa Beta Pi legal sororities, and that's all I cared." One reason for her heavy involvement in the social life of the school, which was atypical of women in part-time schools, "was because my father had already been going there two years." Dr. Mooers, for example, liked to use her father and her for his hypothetical cases in contract law. In a sense, WCL was a second large family for the Salisburys.

The design of the building enhanced this feeling: "It was an old Victorian-style remodeled house with balustrade and a beautiful stairway. On the first floor, right inside, were offices. Each year had a separate room.... I think you were a senior when you got to the first floor. The second floor had sophomores. The third floor had people who were entering. Then they built a library on the top floor. "The classrooms were big, long rooms with flat floors. The building backed up to a hotel, and occasionally couples would check into that hotel and forget to pull the blinds. The professor would lose his class.... We'd occasionally call the hotel and say, "Would you please ask those people to pull their blinds?"

Elizabeth was the self-described child of the class. Most of her classmates were in their thirties, forties, or fifties, and were in a government career where they realized they couldn't go any farther without a law degree. "We each had our own individual chair with an arm on it and a place for you to put your books.... I always sat on the end of the row, and there was a coterie of five men who sat around me with the understanding that they would help me if I would take notes in shorthand and type [them] up."

As with other WCL students, Dr. Mooers stood out among Elizabeth's teachers. But with Elizabeth he became part of the family theme. "He looked a great deal like my father; he was a slender New Englander. He gave the best advice [for exam-taking] of anybody that I heard. '[The] thing... people are going to be interested in is not whether you give the right answer.... They want to know how you can support the answer you give.... So if you're stuck, you take a piece of paper, write down all the reasons for, and [on the other] all the reasons against, and you pick which one you think is best, and then you make your argument that way.... Don't try to argue both ways, because then they'll really find out how little you know.' "

Dr. Mooers's advice proved helpful for the bar exam, which Elizabeth passed on her first try in 1935. "The curriculum at the Washington College of Law prepared you to take the D.C. bar exam all the way through. At first they threw in a little of Maryland and Virginia because they knew people would be practicing in those jurisdictions too—I think that's one reason they didn't use the case method system so much. Georgetown and George Washington used those methods. Of course they were preparing people to take the bar anywhere in the United States. And were so geared. As a result WCL for years had the highest number of graduates who passed the bar the first time."

Despite the fact that WCL students came from across the nation, "they were going to stay here. It was before World War II and before mobility and all the things that we have these days. In 1935 another friend of mine graduated from law school at the University of Montana. He had gotten himself a government job in Washington. . . . He packed all his worldly goods in a straw suitcase, put on a straw hat, and went to Washington to take a job. And in the 30's you didn't come in expecting you were going to get some high salary because you had a law degree. In the government those days the only way you got anywhere was to take a Grade 1 job which paid $1260 a year and work your way up, and you didn't transfer around among agencies, because if you did they assumed there was something wrong with you. So anyone with a law degree who came to Washington, or was in Washington, got himself a Grade 1 file clerk job in an agency that he thought he'd like to spend the rest of his life in." It was the same for a man as a woman. "He started from the bottom, and hoped somebody would transfer or die."

Elizabeth didn't follow this track. "I was working with the Treasury and then I went to the Civil Service Commission for six months and then Social Security" in 1938. While at Civil Service, she decided to stop commuting back and forth to Virginia and to "leave the nest." "I said to my father, 'Pop, I just can't stand those little kids anymore.' He said, 'I know what you mean.' So I got myself a one-room apartment in Washington, and then I broke the news to my mother. [She had a really violent reaction and] didn't speak to me for two or three weeks." It wasn't that her mother needed the help: "she didn't approve of me going off by myself."

Unlike a female friend, who had had to wait for World War I to get a government job because of strict quotas on the number of employees from a particular state, Elizabeth entered government in the world of FDR's "alphabet agencies." Though she, like many applicants was from Virginia, the Roosevelt administration "brought people in by the hundreds and they sort of blinked their eyes at the state quotas and lots of other things." Still, she had had to wait for her Civil Service Commission job—from 1930, when she first took the test, until 1936, when she got it.

1940 brought Elizabeth not only a masters degree from WCL, but her first "professional job." Her supervisor at Social Security, a Miss Halsey, made her the attorney in charge of unemployment compensation decisions. "We'd get the decisions in from outgoing compensation boards. We wrote headnotes and the index and then we indexed them into a master index, which we updated every six months. All the men in the office were either in the Reserve or . . . the National Guard, or they were drafted or something. [They] all kept going into the service, and told me to keep things running just as they had been until their return. And eventually I became the unit chief in charge of putting together and publishing a summary of IRS rulings affecting unemployment compensation. You had to have a law degree in order to have the job."

Elizabeth, ever restless, decided to join the Navy after a tiff with her supervisor over pay and promotion. After training at Smith College, she became Ensign Salisbury, but not in the Judge Advocate General's Corps. "In World War II women didn't think of going into the JAG. They might think about doing it, but it's not the same as doing it. The Coast Guard [with whom Helene Lawrence, Portia '39, served], was better for women. For women, Coast Guard was tops." But Elizabeth didn't enlist in the Coast Guard when she had the chance, because her brother had become disenchanted with the attitude at the Coast Guard Academy and left. In the Navy, she did personnel work in the Bureau of Ships and eventually accepted an assignment with the Selective Service Reserve in 1950, after post-war employment with the Social Security Board and Veteran's Administration.

Much of Elizabeth Salisbury's job–hopping was based on her feeling that she was not being promoted fast enough. When she left the Social Security Board, she had been doing a Grade 7 job at Grade 5 rank and pay. "Every man who came back [from the war] got a promotion." To Elizabeth her bosses said, "We're sorry, but we've run out of money." Then the Veteran's Administration offered her a substantial promotion, to Grade 12. This came about with considerable difficulty. The man involved (at VA) had told two of her friends (one a sorority sister), who were trying to convince him to take Elizabeth, that "a woman's place is in the home." However, they persuaded him that she would be a valuable employee because of all the women veterans the VA would suddenly have to deal with after the war. "So he said, 'All right, but if she causes any trouble, remember it was your idea.'

Now, that was the attitude towards women when I was working there." This had not been true in the Navy during the war, "but of course the Navy needed people [then]."

At Selective Service, Elizabeth became a full-fledged lawyer, fifteen years out of law school. "I got to go into the United States District Court and help the U.S. Attorney [with cases she knew about]." But basically she was still in a supporting role.

Marriage came late for Elizabeth: "The problem was a dearth of applicants. . . . In the first place I was working in an office where all the men were married. I went to law school at night. . . . I didn't meet a single unmarried man in law school that I know of. I was working with the sorority, which was all women. When I went into Selective Service in the 1950's, General Hershey's requirement for being a male member of the Reserve was you had to be over 35 . . . and married . . . a pillar in the community. And so I would go to camp once every two years with a hundred men, all of whom were married. So I operated in an aura where there weren't too many possibilities. I was working eight hours a day for the government, I was working pretty nearly eight hours a day for the sorority, [and] I was organist in the church." Elizabeth's one serious romance was with a fourth cousin from Connecticut, to whom she was briefly engaged.

"He came down several times, and I didn't like the way he presented the ring. . . . I got lost [in a parade] one day, and I used a swear word, and he informed me that ladies don't swear, and he told me that when I came up to Connecticut we were going to have this house, and it was going to look like this, and we were going to have four children, and these were the children's names. Once a month he [said he] would let me take his car . . . and drive to Hartford [to] see my grandfather. Well, I had had my own car for ten years."

After staying with the VA for twelve years at Grade 12, and being told by her boss that he was holding a Grade 13 job for a man, Elizabeth finally married John Denny, who had been offered a management position with the VA. "I said, 'Dear John, I'm never going to get anywhere in this man's world, so I might as well get married,' " which she did at age 51 in 1963. She was hired back as a legal specialist at Grade 14 when the Johnson administration demanded women at that level. Until then, "I was a very important person [at VA], but not important enough to pay." It had been a long, hard road, culminating with Elizabeth's childhood dream, becoming administrative assistant "to a big-shot"—General Hershey of the Selective Service System—near the close of her government career. From 1970 to 1973 she also filled the office of Special Advisor to the President of the United States on

Manpower Mobilization, "with the help of one secretary and one chauffeur." Her last assignment at the Selective Service System was "Assistant to the Deputy Director and General Counsel," with general supervision over 7 field attorneys stationed around the country, assisting U.S. attorneys in prosecuting "draft dodgers."

What kept Elizabeth Denny going throughout her professional life is perhaps best summarized by what she had told a professor from the University of Texas who asked her at a reception for women law students whether, after all, she didn't really believe a woman's place is in the home: "Professor, I have a mother who bore and raised ten children. All the children have gone from the nest and my mother is absolutely aimless. She doesn't have any more purpose in life, and it [has] worked on her. I wish that everybody could have some kind of a profession that they could do after their children grow up. . . ."

Marguerite Rawalt: Network Builder

Another law school in Washington that provided a stepping-stone for women in law was a university school—George Washington, which not only had an evening school, but, unlike Georgetown, admitted women. One of its most prominent female graduates was Marguerite Rawalt, a self-described "Texan."[14]

Born in Illinois, Marguerite went to a junior college in Texas after moving from Wichita, Kansas, where she had spent the first two years of high school. She had a happy, supportive family life. Her father was a farmer and farm-supply salesman, "a man of old-fashioned principles." She remembers him as a workaholic. Her mother was Irish and "had the best disposition of anybody I've ever known." After Marguerite and her two brothers were grown, Mrs. Rawalt went into a dressmaking business in Kingsville, Texas, where Mr. Rawalt was, for the last ten years of his life, superintendent of the huge King Ranch.

Marguerite was very close to her two brothers. The elder, Lewis, enlisted in the Navy at age 18, during the First World War. He came out of the Navy "with one lung and one kidney. . . . He was a sportsman, owning for many years a sporting-goods store on Covey Island in South Texas." Marguerite's younger brother Willis was a farmer, running "rather large farms that my dad had acquired in South Texas . . . and his own farms."

Marguerite's parents expected all the children to be good students, living "by papa's principles. Neither father nor mother encouraged me or originally gave me the idea of becoming a lawyer," but "when I decided to do so they were 100 percent for it."

The decision to go to law school involved several influential people. "My first boss was a woman," the superintendent of schools for Lorena, Texas, where Marguerite taught high-school mathematics—Miss Lucy Anne Moore. Superintendent Moore was "a woman with great strength of character, a disciplinarian, and I grew to adore her ...." Miss Moore left Lorena "to go to Texas University Law School and graduate ... I followed in her footsteps later. When she left, she made me superintendent of schools to succeed her. That was a twelve-grade school [with twelve teachers] and I was hardly 21 years old."

Marguerite subsequently became office manager of a Chevrolet dealership in San Antonio "that did a very large business." Although Miss Moore was a great influence on Marguerite's plans to study law, it was her aggravation at doing all the work for a lawyer who drew a contingency fee from this business which finally drove her to it. This fee "was almost equal to my salary, but when he got ready to make out a paper to foreclose on an automobile or on an account, I had to draft all the facts on it. I said to myself, if he can draw that much money for doing nothing, I'm going to study law."

Finally, Marguerite was influenced by her work as confidential secretary to the governor of Texas for two years. "He was a lawyer, well known all over the state, and highly regarded.... That was a great influence on me, my admiration of his work—he was a man of high principles." However, "he tried to discourage me about studying law. "When I first announced that I would like to study law, he said, 'Now, Rawalt ... you have everything it takes mentally and emotionally to be a good lawyer. But ... I just can't see you in a criminal court prosecuting or defending a rapist.' 'But Governor, there's other law than criminal cases—I wouldn't want to do criminal work."

The governor subsequently went to Washington as a member of the United States Board of Mediation, which handled labor disputes. One day in San Antonio, Marguerite received a wire that said, "Rawalt, here's your chance. You can come to Washington as my secretary and go to a first-class university law school at night." "And so I came to Washington, where I worked as a secretary and went to law school at night."

When she came to Washington, Marguerite announced to a young man in her office that she was going to Georgetown Law School, because Georgetown "was the highest-ranking law school in the city at that time." He and others in the office had "smirks on their faces and they said, 'We don't think you're going to Georgetown . . .' I thought they were challenging my pre-legal work. But of course the fact was that Georgetown did not admit females." Marguerite entered George Washington University instead in the fall of 1930.

At the time, Marguerite Rawalt wasn't particularly aware of discrimination against women in law. "I grew up . . . in a background which accepted the secondary level of women–that the proper roles of women were to be teachers, nurses, clerks, but not the boss. And I think we didn't learn to fight that until the women's movement got active in later years, and I became very active in it." At the time, "there were women lawyers that I knew, [but] there were so few. And as a matter of fact, my father said to me, 'Marguerite, I think you're a damn fool to go to law school, because it's going to require two or three years of education to get your law degree . . . and how are you going to make a living when you get out? Do you think the public is willing to patronize a woman lawyer? I doubt it.' . . . It was all right with him . . . but he was just looking at it in a practical way.

"The case method that was taught in law school was completely new to anybody coming out of the academic world working for a literary degree. It's a completely different way of studying, you know, and it frightened me at first because I took many notes . . . I got very nervous about this in my first year for the reason that the whole thing was going to depend on an examination at the end of the . . . [semester]". So Marguerite went to one of the professors, Professor Moll, and told him of her anxieties. "He said, 'Right over there on that shelf are several ponies. They're narratives. Narrative discussions of these principal cases. Now you can go over there and pick one out and take it home with you, but I warn you that you may not get the help out of it you want. . . . We don't teach in a narrative way.' Some law schools did. Some law schools taught a regular textbook, spelling it all out for you."

During a typical week, Marguerite worked each day for the governor at the Mediation Board from 9 to 5, and then went to law school from 6 to 8. Next she went home and studied. "It was all I could take. Every day I had classes . . . and Saturday and Sunday I studied some more. . . . I can tell you this. I didn't own a TV and I didn't spend time . . . listening to the radio."

Marguerite's Texas connections continued to serve her well. A Texas judge whom she knew, and his wife, helped her settle in an efficiency apartment in a large apartment building they lived in on 16th Street. While living there, working and studying law, Marguerite "ate spasmodically. I would eat out maybe at a cafeteria—go home and fix something on a little grill." She had some social life, "but believe me the law was first."

There were so few women in her law class, Marguerite "thought in a way that we had an advantage. . . . [There were] so few women that they knew us, and the poor boys . . . could never have their names and faces known. . . . I was in a class [of] 220 graduates [and] three or four women." Washington College of Law, one block away from George Washington, was the place most Washington women studied law.

Marguerite liked the way she was treated by the all-male faculty, particularly by an elderly teacher the students called "Daddy Ernest." Professor Ernest taught Marguerite criminal law. "He said to me in a very fatherly, grandfatherly way, 'Now, Miss Marguerite, I want you to know that I will never embarrass you or the other girl in the class by asking you to recite on such a case as a rape case. . . .' I thought that was mighty nice. . . . He was a very thoughtful and dear man."

Social life at the school was limited for Marguerite, much of it involving the international women's law sorority Kappa Beta Pi, which had been founded at Chicago-Kent Law School in 1908. "They took me under their wing, along with the other one or two. They gave me some help on how to study. . . . The women had a good-sized room—it was sort of a rest room—and they would come in to make a cup of tea, and serve us some cookies, those two women, in between classes . . . and of course invite us into their . . . sorority."

After her second year, Marguerite decided to take the bar exam before finishing school. Professor Ernest "called me aside and said, 'Now, Miss Marguerite, I don't think that it's wise to push yourself to take the bar examination.' And I said, 'There's going to be a change of administration [Hoover to Roosevelt] and things are going to change here, and I need the money.' " So she took the bar a year early and passed it, qualifying her to become a lawyer immediately upon her graduation in 1933. There was no employment assistance of any kind from George Washington University. "I had to use as much political pull to get a job as a lawyer after I graduated . . . as I would have [to use] today to get on the Sixth Circuit Court of Appeals! Political pull, think of it, to get a little beginning lawyer's job. . . . I went into the office of the chief counsel of the Internal Revenue Service as an attorney at the lowest level they hired. . . . I had to take a salary cut. As a secretary I got $2800 a year. I went in as a lawyer at $1800."

Taking that job "was a mark of great wisdom on my part. I knew [as her father had warned her] that I probably could not make much of a living as a lawyer in general practice and [friends at Kappa Beta Pi] confirmed this for me. . . . They said, 'That's right, you'll get the divorce cases. You'll get the landlord/tenant cases. And you'll never make a lot of money hanging up your shingle by yourself. There isn't a law firm in the city that would employ you as a partner. They might employ you as a ghostwriter and a researcher, but you would not be a member of the firm.'

"So the government was more likely. It employed a few women. There were not many. I knew them all. But at least the government would employ [women] lawyers . . . and FDR had just been elected. . . . I had to have letters from the politicians of Texas, from the governor, from the chairman of the . . . Texas Democratic Committee and the committee's woman member. On and on. . . . [This] was because I was a woman. There had been, I think, three women in the whole of the Internal Revenue Service . . . and they had gone in politically. One of them had been with the senator from her state and so forth, and they all lost their jobs [with the change of administrations]. I was appointed when the Democrats went in. . . . I think . . . thirty-one lawyers [were] appointed at the headquarters office here. And I, of course, was the only woman. We had a picture, and I stick out like a sore thumb. But it took all of that to get that job."

If it took politics to get even a low-level job, Marguerite reasoned, both her status and that of other women could only be improved through politics and organization: "I joined the Federal Bar Association quickly. That is a national bar association of lawyers who have [worked] for the federal government somewhere. [The] Supreme Court Justices are members of the Federal Bar. They're honorary members, but they participate in our functions. . . . Thus, it "was quite a feat to be elected" president of the Federal Bar Association, in 1942. "I was elected president of the American Association of Women Lawyers in August . . . [1941] and my term ended the next August, and in May 1942, while I was still president of the American Association, I was elected president of the Federal Bar Association, which was 95 percent [male].

"There was a handful of women, about five of us, in the Federal Bar Association, and they said, 'Well, now, Marguerite, you've been coming up the line. You were third vice-president, second vice-president.' The way we did it was never to let the men know that we women were working together. We didn't want any sex segregation idea in it at all. We operated in secret. . . . They decided I'd be the one [who advanced]."

"And so Lucy Howarth, who was on the Board of Veterans' Appeals, would talk to all the men she worked with, and say, 'Marguerite's a good person. We ought to have one woman. You guys ought to recognize a woman, and she's a good one. . . .' So I got elected third vice-president. You were elected up the line. But when they put me up for the presidency, I had opposition all along the line. When it came to the presidency, they really put on quite a regular political ball. I got eighty-something percent of the votes, though. They couldn't find a strong man to run against me.

"I had done a good job as third and second and first vice-president. . . . They couldn't find anything against that. . . . There hasn't been a woman president since." Marguerite held the position for the year's term and then persuaded a fellow Texan, Assistant Attorney General Tom Clark, to run and succeed her. Clark later became an Associate Justice of the United States Supreme Court and was the father of a recent Attorney General, Ramsey Clark. In the meantime, Marguerite remained with Internal Revenue, "working up the line" for thirty years.

By the time she retired, Marguerite had reached the highest position ever attained by a woman at IRS—assistant head of the litigation division of the Office of Chief Counsel. This division tried all tax cases in the federal district courts all over the country. "The division handled all those cases from Washington. We supervised [lawyers across the country]." Marguerite appeared in court often.

In 1961, John F. Kennedy appointed Marguerite Rawalt to the President's Commission on the Status of Women. This began a decided shift in her activities away from professional groups toward those concerned primarily with the advancement of women. She served on the Commission until 1969, analyzing those laws which affected women differently from men and making recommendations for their change. At the same time, she chaired the Task Force on Women's Civil and Political Rights and served on other national committees concerned with the status of women.

After retiring from Internal Revenue, Marguerite was contacted by Betty Friedan and other leaders of the women's movement. As a result, when the National Organization for Women (NOW) was organized in 1966, she was named its general counsel. In that capacity she handled the appeal of the first case that had been lost by a woman "on the assembly line" under Title VII of the Civil Rights Act of 1964. Next she joined the board of Women's Equity Action League, "an activist group. I was on the board from the beginning, and so ever since that time that's all I've done. I haven't been a tax lawyer since." In fact, Marguerite did much more. As a member and former president of the National Federation of Business and Professional Women's Clubs, which had supported the Equal Rights Amendment since the 1940's, and as a member of the Women's Bureau under President

Kennedy, Marguerite spent a good deal of time, beginning in the 1960's, promoting ERA.

Yet this phenomenally active woman found time for marriage, if not for children. In 1936 she married a major in the Army Air Corps who became superintendent of Boeing Field Air Base, predecessor of the important Andrews Air Force Base outside Washington. She managed to combine marriage to a military man with her professional life, "I guess because the Major put up with it. We did a lot of traveling. We both loved the automobile and we had quite an active social life." There "were many weekends in the winter . . . when I was working away at my desk at home . . . and he would be listening to the football games and the like. But I did an awful lot of traveling [alone] while I was president of the National Federation. . . . [It] had 170,000 members and we had [a number of] clubs and state federations, and so the president is a busy person." Thus, for the duration of her two-year term, "the Major, he'd call the travel agent and say, [e.g.,] 'Marguerite has to go to Missoula, Montana [for the weekend].' "

A key reason for Marguerite Rawalt's success apparently lay in her deep affection for her chosen career. "I think that I had a profession that's just tops. I loved every bit of it, and especially tax law. It's fascinating, because in tax law you get [into] every other branch of law. You're dealing with corporate law. . . . You have to deal with probate law because [of estate taxes]. There'll be all sorts of cases involving salaried and employed people and their taxability, and you simply get it all—even criminal law. . . ." Women lawyers today "have a marvelous profession, but they've got to be good at it. . . . You've got to be able to really, really work . . . at law. It's not a place to go to hunt a husband."

*****

Nadine Lane Gallagher: Professional Success through the Washington Women's Network

Born in Little Rock, Arkansas, Nadine Lane Gallagher lived in Texas as a child and before her parents separated she traveled around with them quite a good deal before coming to Washington with her mother and grandmother at about 10 years of age.[15] "My grandfather was the first Episcopal clergyman to be ordained in Arkansas, and so I enjoyed traveling on my grandfather's ecclesiastical coattails when I happened to be in that state. . . . He was an Episcopal pioneer, a missionary." Quite in contrast was her life in the nation's capital, which she loved for its beauty, its "trees and wide avenues." There she attended a large public high school, "which had excellent teachers." Nadine recalled that "many of its graduates turned out to be generals, doctors, lawyers and judges. . . ."

Nadine's education, however, did not follow traditional lines. "[M]y mother was a very charming and intellectual lady, so that at an early age I was more or less amenable to the learning process. My husband, whom I married shortly after high school, was much older than I. He was a very brilliant writer, historian, newspaper man and lived in China—in Shanghai . . . [He] was a magnificent mentor, and to him I owe much of my directional development. Frankly, I feel that I have a universal, if not university education, because my husband was writing political articles, and so I would listen to discussions with knowledgeable people, some of whom subsequently became important officials in China. I would curl up in the corner of the library while they were talking about international affairs. I was drinking it all in. And I went with my husband to various unusual places, because he thought I ought to learn about them. So I did have a very exceptional education." Though separated from her father, Nadine was still able to benefit from the guidance of a mature man.

Nadine had never given any thought to attending law school until "a happy accident led up to my decision. When I returned from the Orient, my husband was invited to make a talk at the Women's City Club, which was a very large club in Washington. The president was Judge Mary O'Toole, one of the early [women] judges of the District of Columbia. As I was the wife of the speaker I was invited to be a member of the club. . . . This club had been organized by very able and prominent professional women doctors, lawyers, bankers, accountants, civic leaders, and people who were doing important things. . . . In my heart of hearts I've always been sort of a hero worshipper [of] people who do things for others. [T]he president of the club, Grace Hayes Riley, had just been appointed the dean of Washington College of Law . . . She said, 'Nadine, why don't you come to law school?' And I looked up at her—she was a very imposing, attractive woman—and I blinked a little bit, and I said, 'Well, I don't know,' and that was the end of the conversation.

"I went home and said to my husband, 'Mrs. Riley wants me to go to law school.' All he said was, 'Well, why not? You won't do any worse than anybody else.' In other words, he didn't say, 'What do you want to do that for?' . . . No psychological barrier was raised. It was a very casual thing."

Ill health, however, was to cast a shadow over Nadine's early adulthood. "I had a serious attack, at 19, of rheumatoid arthritis. It stayed with me for about twenty-five years. . . . These years were very traumatic because of my own ill health and that of my husband. I went to night school and I worked all day. Sometimes I wondered if I was going to be able to get on the [street] car, and get off again. . . . Physical pain. Always in pain." With the care of her mother, Nadine was able to surmount this serious obstacle, which hindered daily living. "[Y]ou just do what needs to be done. And you either make it or you don't. But don't stop to ask why you are doing something when you *must* do something. Just do it."

Asked what she thought law school would be like, Nadine replied: "I didn't think. I went to school. It was another intellectual pursuit. . . . I had a responsibility of a monetary nature that I would have to be able to meet. . . . Like all the rest of the people in Washington going to night school, I was not going for the fun of it, but because I wanted to learn something. All were making personal sacrifices of time and money and energy. And that's what night school's about in Washington."

Of her teachers at Washington College of Law, two in particular stand out: "One of the most famous teachers was Ed Mooers, an unusually gifted lecturer . . . eventually lecturer emeritus. . . . He was a delightful person, in every fashion. And very friendly. He was a marvelous teacher." The other was Elizabeth Harris who taught torts. "She was a Massachusetts woman, I think. She usually wore rather mannish suits and one time she came to . . . school with a string of beads and everybody thought she looked lovely. [It was unusual] because she was very businesslike. . . . I liked her very much, but I never knew her that well.

It was at this time that a story was circulating about of the first woman who was admitted to the bar of the Supreme Court. Striped trousers and cutaways were then the proper attire for men. I don't know who this woman was . . . but she ordered a suit with a striped skirt and a cutaway jacket, for her admission to the Supreme Court to conform with protocol. Some of the women of that time were still finding it advisable not to be too 'frou-frou' in court. And they were almost forced into a role that was not necessarily themselves. They were not accepted then with noticeable warmth."

A member of Phi Delta Delta legal sorority, Nadine eventually became president of it. The contacts made at that time have proved enduring. "In Washington we still have a group of Beta chapter members. . . . We have a very delightful luncheon or dinner from time to time at one of the nice hotels. . . . I keep in touch with a good many of them."

Upon graduation, Nadine, like other legal sorority members, sought to continue her formal networking by joining the Women's Bar Association. "In the early 1940's the District of Columbia Bar Association had just opened its doors to women, presumably because many of the lawyers had gone to war, and presumably they could do with some more members." However, Nadine did not join at first. "It was still an unusual situation. Negroes and women [had been excluded]. Women got that a little sooner than [their] black brethren. It shows you how prejudiced people can be.

"I first joined the Women's Bar Association which was organized in 1924. Shortly thereafter I found myself president. I never quite knew why. And that again was a sort of a casual thing.... There was a very low ebb in membership. In fact, it was so low that we couldn't even elect a nominating committee. [But] the system was very good. So some of us were having coffee in the lounge of the hotel, and somebody says, 'Why don't you be president?' And I said, 'Heavens no!' And that was the end of it as far as I was concerned. However, two days later I began to get some telephone calls, and I thought, 'Well, it's at a pretty low ebb, it might be kind of fun.' So I was president of that for two years, and we did get it up to about four hundred members when I left."

With the admission of women into the "men's bar ... there wasn't a need for a separate women's association. Fortunately, there were some very wise women among them who knew that it's the concerted effort of people—men or women—that counts with the public. You will just be crying in the wilderness unless you have others with you. Women lawyers belong to both organizations; however it is the concerted voice of the Women's Bar Association that is heard by the public.

"In the "men's bar, ... you were just a member of a committee of a thousand gentlemen ... but nobody listened.... You were not in the power structure. Now I am happy to say that many of our women lawyers from the bar association have had recognition as members of the board and so on. It's been long in coming, of course."

While serving in a non-legal job in the Legal Department of the Federal Reserve, Nadine sat for and passed a special Civil Service exam for lawyers. "I went with the Selective Service and very proudly; those of us who were just out of law school, we had the magnificent sum of $2,000 a year, which was better than $1,800 [her Federal Reserve Salary]! And it was rather interesting, we were really reviewing presidential appeals for exemption from the draft, and I expected to be there for possibly a year. However, this was during the war, you see, and six months later we were told that they were reducing the status of the job from professional to administrative....

"There were only two of us who decided we were going to cling tenaciously to our professional standing. As low as it was, we were not going to give it up. So I went over to the Department of Justice because some of the girls had gone over there and said, 'Now, you go over and see Mr. So-'n'-so.' So I went and saw Mr. So-'n'-So, and it so happens I got the job, which turned out to be very, very interesting to me. The section was small had public relations aspects to it. We worked with U.S. Government legal divisions and the Council of State Governments to facilitate the war effort by modifying state laws and/or introducing new ones. So it was interesting, and that's where I was when I was appointed [to the District of Columbia bench] by President Truman."

Discussing the effect of World War II on jobs in Washington, Nadine had the following observations. "The war opened the door for women, just as many women got jobs in the First World War because they needed people to do things. [T]he women lawyers were needed in regulatory departments and it was often a matter of interpreting and writing legal regulations and so on. The Department of Justice had a great many very fine women lawyers. Of course, there was Mabel Walker Willebrandt in the very early days following World War I; [she] distinguished herself as an Assistant Deputy Attorney General in charge of the Prohibition enforcement. She brought in several very fine women in to the tax department.... They belonged to the Women's Bar Association and my legal sorority and so on. So it was interesting to see that through these organizations, women were able to be part of the legal profession. Again, there are always those, I suppose, who don't need the assistance of their fellows, but I think most of us need the support of one another."

The appointment to the bench by President Truman in 1946 came as a surprise to Nadine Gallagher. "I had no interest in being a judge. I was called up to the [Attorney General's] office and I thought they just wanted to discuss some of those women who had their applications in. So I said to the gentleman ... 'What can I do for you?' And he said, 'I want to talk to you about the judgeships.' ... I thought he wanted to know who was cooperative, who among the group you could rely upon, and if you're president of an organization you know who is going to do the job and who is going to promise to do it and then not do it.... Then he said, 'We were thinking of you.' So with that I was nonplussed. There was a deep silence, and he turned to me and he said, 'Well?' I came out with a very corny reply. I said,

'Well . . . obviously this is an honor which any lawyer would be very much interested in and concerned [with] and so forth,' . . . and said without any reason, 'Well, I haven't been a member of the bar for very long, but I'm legal.' So he asked a few questions, and I said, 'Well, I can't tell you now, because I must think this over very carefully.' And he said, 'Well, I'd like to know as soon as possible.' It was on a weekend, and I said: 'Will the first part of the week be all right?' . . . He said, 'Yes—make it Monday if you can!'

Caught by surprise, Nadine was at first "considerably shaken" by the offer. "I went home and said to my mother—I hink I burst into tears; and she asked, 'What's the matter, dear?' And I said, 'They want me to be a judge, and I don't want to be a judge; I don't want to live in a goldfish bowl.'

" 'Well, why don't you take it, and if you don't like it, give it back to them?' She didn't want her only daughter to be unhappy, you see. . . . That was like cold water on my fevered brow and I thought, 'My heavens, the war is about over and this office that I am in is [the] War Policy Division of the Department of Justice. Any law [job] would be disappearing; I'd better give this some very serious thought and come to terms with myself.' Which of course I did."

Questioned on why she had never given any thought to becoming a judge, Nadine laughingly gave an answer reflecting her judicial demeanor. "Don't ask me a 'why' question because you'll only get an argumentative answer! And I never would have permitted that in court. . . . When you say 'why,' it's a speculative question and I think speculation is sort of worthless, it's like an opinion. . . . Why didn't I think about becoming a judge? I don't know, I don't have the answer to that. I was doing what I [do] today—I still practice this: today is the only thing I have, and the only thing you have, so I make a reasonable plan of the future—so that you can pay the rent, and do what you want to do and buy yourself a new dress, take a trip and so forth and so on. But as to why I never thought about a judgeship, I don't think—I obviously didn't want it. Simple as that. . . . You have to be provident, don't mistake me; but I have never sought a material pot of gold from any rainbow."

On managing a work life and a home life, Nadine was pragmatic: "[I did] whatever had to be done. I managed it by going to bed, eating, getting up in the morning, going to work, studying. . . . But I never projected or thought about something that was detrimental because I couldn't do what I had to do and worry at the same time."

Judge Gallagher's outlook on life coincided well with President Truman's, as she found when she visited Mr. Truman to pay her respects after becoming a judge. "I was surprised I couldn't find something more original to say, but I said: 'Mr. President, at the risk of being very trite . . . I must say that you certainly carry those heavy burdens in a very gallant and pleasant fashion.' And he said, 'Well, it's like this: when I got this job, I made up my mind I couldn't work 'n' worry at the same time, so I'd just work.' And I've never forgotten that, and I've never failed to pass it on."

While Nadine worked and attended her hospitalized husband, the court's other judges "didn't pay much attention to me. What I mean is, I didn't know them intimately. . . . [Y]ou never know what goes on in another judge's chambers, of course, or in his courtroom . . . so you're pretty much on your own. The men would go to lunch—we had no regular lunchroom in this lovely courthouse. . . so they'd go to the drugstore or somewhere and chat among themselves. I'm not easily intimidated, but I don't barge in, you see, which I think sometimes is a mistake. However, [it] depends on who you are and how you manage yourself. So I usually had my lunch in my chambers. I lived on sandwiches for about ten years because I never went out to lunch. During that period there was always a time when somebody wanted you to sign a paper. Everybody else was having lunch, so some lawyers would say, 'Judge, would you just sign this?' So he could go to lunch! Well, I was a public servant, so I never complained."

Judge Gallagher has been asked to speak to many people about her career in law. "I referred to it facetiously as a 'happy accident!' I have had occasion to talk [at] law days and [to] parents and young people [who] come and talk to me about law school. I tell them what I think the law is about. It isn't all about making money. You're in a profession, you're not in a skilled trade; and I draw the distinction philosophically and practically. So I can always say, if you don't really know what you want to do with your life and you don't want to go to work yet, you would profit by the discipline . . . the mental exercise, but particularly [from] the discipline and the knowledge that is there. If you do discipline yourself, that will serve you forever in your life. Every man and woman who goes to law school, or even passes the bar, is not necessarily a lawyer. [However,] you are well trained in the law, and it should be used to your advantage and the advantage of others. That is what I believe.

"You see, I'm very much a 'people' person—I like men people, and lady people, and nice people, and small people. . . . I'm not too keen about dull people! But I am an advocate, and I've had occasion to make talks on many subjects, including the status of women in this area where I'm now living because there are a great many very intelligent women there, many of whom have never made a living. They're beneficiaries of trust funds, wealthy husbands and fathers and so on, and active in philanthropic activities [and] civic affairs.

"But there's a difference [when] you relate to people who must make their living to pay the rent, to take care of the children, the ill husband, the ancient parents.... So I have had occasion to say to my friends, 'I'm not concerned with myself, or you, or you—but I am concerned about the legal status of and attitudes toward any [woman] who has to go out and make a living to take care of somebody and their family.' I abhor the discrimination that they have had to suffer from time to time, and still do. They're subtle discriminations—the pat on the knee for the woman who has to pay the rent, who has to have a job to take care of her children. She doesn't know what to do.

"As our friend Phyllis Shoe-Fly, Schafly, whatever her name is (I call her Shoe-Fly), said at one point, and I think it was a mistake, 'The virtuous woman doesn't have any problems of that kind.' I thought, 'Lady, the woman who is familiar with the business world knows how to handle such things. It is the naive, inexperienced woman with a family to support who should be protected from sex harassment when she desperately needs to hold onto her job. They're the ones I'm interested in'."

Just before she retired from the bench in 1957, Nadine extended her networks worldwide by visiting Asia as a "specialist in law" in connection with the International Exchange Program of the State Department. Her travels brought her full circle from her trips as a young wife and renewed a number of old acquaintances. Since she was traveling as a representative of the U.S. Government, Nadine was given royal treatment. Despite her concern for the underdog, Nadine noted, "There's nothing wrong with the red carpet if you're on it."

5

Chicago: Go West Young Woman, But Not to Practice Law

CHICAGO-KENT LAW SCHOOL AND THE CHICAGO BAR

In the post-Civil-War period of the nineteenth century, Chicago, then little more than a booming frontier town, played a major role in the entrance of women into law. In June of 1870, Ada H. Kepley, graduating from Chicago's Union College of Law, was the first American woman to earn a law degree.[1] In the same year, Myra Bradwell, who had apprenticed in her husband's office, attempted to become a member of the Illinois bar. The bar's refusal to admit her was to become a celebrated legal case.

Myra Bradwell was already well known at the time she applied for admission. In 1868 she had started the *Chicago Legal News,* the first weekly law periodical in the West. Her husband, a judge and legislator, had used his influence to get a special charter so that she could head the business without the legal handicaps of a married woman. The *Chicago Legal News* was an enormous success, and Ms. Bradwell used it as a vehicle for reforming the court system.[2]

In 1870, the Illinois Supreme Court denied her a license to practice, noting that as a married woman she would not be bound by express or implied contracts. In addition, the court said that although the relevant statute was not specific as to whether women could practice, the legislature had not contemplated, upon its enactment, the admission of women.[3] Only Ms. Bradwell's side argued the case before the Supreme Court, where the majority held, in 1872, that since the right to practice law was not one of the "privileges and immunities" that belong to the citizens of the United States, she could be denied admission.[4] In concurrence, Justice Bradley wrote: "The paramount destiny and mission of women are to fulfill the noble and benign offices of wife and mother. And the rules of civil society must be adopted to the general constitution of things, and cannot be based upon exceptional cases."[5]

Undaunted, Myra Bradwell secured in the same year the passage of an Illinois statute abolishing discrimination in employment. She never practiced law, but through her publishing and legislative work won the respect of bar and bench. In 1890 after the legislature had specifically passed enabling legislation and four years before Ms. Bradwell's death, the Illinois Supreme Court undertook on its own motion to admit this distinguished woman to the bar.[6] The *Chicago Legal News* continued the fight for equality for women throughout the nineteenth century.

By the turn of the century, Chicago was no longer a boom town, but a major industrial city, beginning to rival in influence its much older Eastern counterparts. With prominence came the organization of an establishment bar. Two law schools, both of which admitted women—Chicago and Northwestern—led the way. But the tides of immigration that were sweeping the East also touched Chicago. Masses of Eastern European immigrants arrived in the burgeoning city, setting off predictable responses in its WASP citizens. Yet the children of these immigrants wanted to advance in life; soon part-time law schools sprang up to help them.

The Chicago Evening Law School was founded in 1887 by working young lawyers who wanted more education than apprenticeship could provide them and who had begun studying after work with a judge. In 1888, quarters other than a judge's office were secured, and the name of the institution was changed to the Chicago College of Law. Classes were scheduled for 6:30 P.M., a time which was found to suit best the convenience of both students and instructors.[7]

In 1889 the college became the law department of Lake Forest University, which it remained until the dissolution of the university in 1904. From its beginning, the school required three years of legal education—instead of the two mandated by the state—before conferring its law degree. Its growth was so rapid that larger quarters were secured in 1892 in the Atheneum Building on Van Buren Street, which were occupied until the college moved in 1912 to several (noncontiguous) floors in the Lake View Building on South Michigan Avenue. The school remained there for eleven years.[8]

In 1900 the Kent College of Law, which had been founded in 1892 and which was the second largest school in the state, merged with Chicago College of Law and the name of the school was changed to Chicago-Kent College of Law. Three other institutions were then merged into Chicago-Kent: the Western College of Law in 1912; the Chicago Business Law School in 1917; and the Webster College of Law in 1923. When it moved into its new building at 10 North Franklin in 1924,[9] Chicago-Kent had obtained the distinction of being not only the first evening law school in the nation, but one of the largest. In that year—in response to a new requirement that two years of college was necessary for admission to the bar in addition to law school—Chicago-Kent instituted a junior college.[10]

The law school soon found this innovation unnecessary. Illinois, like other Midwestern states, provided public higher education, which allowed sufficient numbers of students to obtain two years of college before entering law school. Also, this emphasis on higher education carried over to private colleges enrolling the non-elite much sooner than was the case in Boston. Still, Chicago-Kent was embroiled in the same struggle with elite law schools as was Portia and WCL. In 1920, the school's students excoriated the AALS recommendation that evening schools be abolished as "an insult" to an institution which has had "such a powerful influence in molding the legal profession."[11]

Chicago-Kent enrolled—on the average—very few women. These women found that they needed support and founded in 1908 the first legal sorority in the United States—Kappa Beta Pi. The sorority was soon flourishing throughout the United States—particularly in Washington, D.C.—and had chapters abroad.

The Chicago-Kent *Review,* which in its early years was primarily a register of social activities rather than a law review, regularly ran in the 1920's both news of Kappa Beta Pi and a section called "The Woman's Page." Items in the *Review* and in the school yearbook *(The Transcript)* provide a revealing glimpse of women's place both as students and alumnae during these years.

A 1922 edition of *The Transcript* noted that "in 3 pleasant years, some girls had come and some girls had gone, but the Misses Agnes B. Clohesy [later radio director for station WCFL, Chicago] and Blanche B. Aronin [interview to follow] had persistently remained throughout the entire course. The congenial personality of these two young ladies naturally encouraged everyone of their fellow classmates toward an ideal . . . [presumably of how dignified lawyering could be]."[12]

Shortly thereafter, the *Review* announced that President Harding had appointed a Beta member from Kent as the first woman attorney on the Board of Indiana Commissioners. Also announced was that Blanche Aronin had become the youngest attorney in Illinois. Finally featured was Hermana Belle Deiches, "former Columbia University girl, who gave us a program of folk songs. Unless you have heard this Texas songbird, you are missing something. She warbles as easily and naturally as she talks and no one would dispute the fact that Hermana can talk."[13]

What we would surely label as sexism today apparently was commonplace. On a subsequent "Woman's Page" in the *Review* appeared the following: "Was Miss Cavanaugh's A in criminal law due to her proficiency in criminology or vampology? We believe the latter to be the probable cause." And another woman in the class was described thus: "The boys in the southeast corner of the room are giving 'Crisp' attention these days."[14]

Taking a more serious tack, the April 1927 *Review* (in its sorority section) featured a comment on "Agnes Clohesy's excellent address on the Workmen's Compensation Act. A member of the sorority, she was generous enough to formulate and condense extensive experience . . . with the Legal Aid Bureau in order that those who are just starting out will be less baffled by the statutes."[15] Likewise, the November issue cited two alumnae working in private practice, a third with "a firm of patent attorneys," a fourth "associated" with another small firm, and a fifth "employed in the Legal Department of the Illinois Central Railroad."[16] Whether "associated with" or "employed in" meant what it generally did for a man is anybody's guess, but the times didn't often provide a woman lawyer equal status with a man.

The same issue contained a bit of theoretical justification for the sorority:

> [She] stands supreme and guards her women. At one time such a fort was necessary to [our] pioneers—but now [the sorority] has become a modern, progressive movement. To the student it extends a confidence, assurance, and support; while to alumnae it retains and harbors unity, friendship and encouragement.[17]

Apparently, some idea of female networking in the profession was taking hold. The year 1929 revealed even more activism among Kappa Beta Pi women, who had "taken to politics" after graduation:

> Irene McCormick, Bertha Carlson and Mrs. Sullivan gave speeches and made themselves generally useful in the cause of putting women on juries, while Irene and Bertha campaigned the state for the same cause, and as we all know, were successful. . . . Mrs. Carlson was invited by the Vocational Director of the University of Illinois to speak to women students on 'Law as a Profession for Women.'[18]

Still, many talented Kent graduates had to find outlets for their feminism in fields much more customary for women than law. An example was Minna Schmidt, '24, lecturer at the University of Chicago and director of the costume workshop there:

> A group of 400 figurines of the best known women in the world, designed and costumed by her, will be [exhibited] at the Century of Progress in Chicago next year. She now has a book in preparation on the 400 greatest women of the world.[19]

"The Woman's Page" of the January 1928 *Review* contained some interesting byplay, written by an unmarried woman law student, commenting on the well-known sacrifices of her married counterparts. "Not having husbands," she began, "we cannot compete with our energetic sisters in cementing the basement floor prior to awakening 'lord' husband and placing before him a breakfast only fit for one bearing his title." Instead, "Our own contribution . . . is Miss Grape, who teaches school five days a week, attends Chicago-Kent classes five nights a week, and is taking a postgraduate history course at the University of Chicago."[20]

A sampling of yearbook quotations about Chicago-Kent's women also helps set the stage for the interviews to follow. Thus it was said of a University of Michigan graduate, "We are charmed with her manner and astounded at her learning";[21] of the class secretary, 1923–25, "a full, rich nature, free to trust, truthful and almost sternly just, impulsive, earnest, prompt to act, makes her generous to a fault";[22] and of a University of Chicago graduate and women's editor of the *Review,* "A charming, darling little maid often mischievous, but never afraid."[23] Edna Cronin (pseudonym), whose interview follows, was termed both "a regular fellow"[24] and "everybody's sweetheart"[25] in the same volume, an ambivalent status perhaps symbolic of that held by many women in law at the time.

Chicago-Kent female students had to be models of mental health just to escape schizophrenia. After all, the school was "truly a big fraternity, and Sisters Davenport, Hughes, McCormack, and McCurdy are just as good fellows as ever cocked a gun."[26] At the same time, another woman student was described as "A Good Cook (line forms on the right)."[27] Perhaps the resolution of these roles could be found in the description, "Going to be a hundred percent helpmate."[28] Still, despite their multifaceted talents, Kent women were told "in jest," "The penalty for bigamy is two wives."[29]

From time to time, Kent female students had the occasion, both in the *Review* and the yearbook, to discuss openly their difficulties in a male-dominated legal profession.

Entitled "Co-Education in the Law," a 1925 article began by asserting that "the history of co-education everywhere shows [that] one of the first obstacles encountered [is] the theory of the mental inferiority of women." Thus, "the first stage of co-education was not without its stimulus. Something had to be proven. Every recitation, every act, was in evidence." [Male] "opposition [was] a greater stimulus than sufferance. When overcome, it is forgiven, even forgotten."[30]

By 1925, "the results of co-education have proven beyond a doubt, the ability of the formerly so-called weaker sex creditably to sustain courses of study hitherto deemed suitable for men only." No difficulties had arisen from putting young women on equal footing with young men in the universities, "and their average scholarship is certainly as high as that of young men."[31]

The bulk of the article then recited the observations of deans and other spokesmen at various law schools about women's ability to compete academically with men. These comments came from the law schools of Southwestern University in Los Angeles; Yale (women admitted 1918); the University of Chicago (women admitted from its founding in 1902); the University of Texas (women admitted from founding in 1883, but first enrolled in 1911); the University of Buffalo; Boston University (women admitted 1872); Pennsylvania; National University in Washington, D.C. (one of the first women ever admitted to a bar, Belva Lockwood, graduated in 1871); and the University of Wisconsin. These correspondents all ranked women as high as or higher than their male counterparts in academic accomplishment. Finally, the article cited experience at the law schools of the Universities of Denver, Cincinnati, and California (Hastings), and at the Kansas City School of Law; at all these institutions, recent classes had women at the very top.[32]

The article's author, Chicago-Kent student Mae Viner, acknowledged, however, that despite this record, "there are still a number of law schools which do not admit women":

> As long as women are admitted to the bar, they should be given equal opportunities with young men to obtain a legal education. We think it has been proven that women possess the same vigor of thought . . . and are as capable of mastering the same legal subjects, as men.[33]

Furthermore, legal education was valuable to women, just as it was to men. In fact, "it is of prime importance in the complete education of every human being." It affords "unequalled mental discipline and tends to make the mind more reasonable, consistent, logical and well-balanced." It is "as useful to women as to men, whether they apply the knowledge to the practice of law or to any other vocation."[34]

Miss Viner recognized that "women have labored under great disadvantages in getting started in practice. They have not been given the opportunities for admission into law firms that have been accorded to men with the same records." Thus "their foothold . . . in the profession has been something striven for and secured by sheer dint of earnest endeavor."[35]

It should be remembered that, at the time Miss Viner wrote, there were only about 1750 women lawyers and judges in the United States. That she was able to point to notable ones like Florence Allen of the Supreme Court of Ohio, Mabel Walker Willebrandt, U.S. Assistant Attorney General, and Mary Bartelme, Judge of the Cook County Superior Court, was cause for optimism. Also, "women are just beginning to find their place in politics . . . as legislators, senators, judges and governors. . . . Legal education is the best route to such offices."[36]

Optimism echoed from the young student's final paragraph:

> The prospect in the future is brighter than in the past, as the old prejudices are melting away and people are putting their trust in professional women more and more. Through conscientious, intelligent work, women are demanding and obtaining recognition by bench and bar. . . . More power to them.[37]

But "more power" did not come easily to women lawyers in the 1920's and 1930's. Another Chicago-Kent female student's article of the period began on a jarring note: "From prehistoric times down through the pages of history women have been man's mere chattel, but with the . . . progress of civilization, laws and habits have been changed until today woman stands on the threshhold of a new era.[38]

"The new woman stands, . . . glorious with the fullness of womanhood, submissive, loving and with the finest instincts of the human race. Not only is she the home maker and mother, but is at once to become a part of our governing forces." Further,

> . . . There is no study which will aid women to become leaders, orators and to acquire intelligence in making our law and voting properly, more than the study of law. The vast majority of women do not want to run this government but, only to cooperate and participate in the making of these laws in which they are so vitally interested for the protection of our boys and girls of the future.[39]

"Why," the writer goes on to ask, should a woman who had the ability "be refused" this chance? "If she takes up the cause for a broader vision and for self education, then it should be to her credit." Though "someone has said, it will destroy our home and take away the refining influence of home life, I do not agree. It will make her have higher ideals and become more intelligent in every phase of life and make better wives, mothers, and citizens and make the profession more respected than it ever had been before *[sic]*."[40]

These remarkable passages reflect the reality that underlay the enthusiasm and optimism of many women in the 1920's. Hidden are any assertions of women's equality in the profession. Instead, the woman lawyer of the future would remain a homemaker and, instead of participating in government on an equal footing with men, would simply "cooperate" in making certain laws.

Women had, it seems, responded to the call to mind their families during difficult times, and to use law not as a full-time career, but to make themselves better homemakers as well as better members of the P.T.A. or League of Women Voters. These were attitudes that did not undergo substantial change until the late 1960's, and should be remembered as the following oral histories unfold.

CHICAGO-KENT COLLEGE OF LAW STUDENTS

Blanche Aronin Lippitz: Organization Woman in Religion

If optimism, regardless of underlying realities, was the prevailing spirit of the woman professional of the 1920's, Blanche Aronin Lippitz epitomized just such an attitude.[41] Born in Russia, Blanche immigrated to this country with her parents at the age of one, eventually settling in Sturgeon Bay, Wisconsin. The eldest of five children, Blanche was strongly influenced by her father in her early years. "He was a teacher. . . . I think my father was the first of a series of men [in his family] who were not rabbis. . . . [For example,] my grandfather was the first rabbi of Sheboygan, Wisconsin. . . . I [like to] think of the people who left [Russia]—what great courage it took, knowing they'd never see their families again, but knowing too that they'd have to come to give their children a proper education."

Education was the central focus of the Aronin family. "We had the kind of family where we studied a great deal. . . . My father would have us sit around the table and discuss [current events]. . . . It was interesting that in our discussions at home we would discuss prophets. That led us all into the area of social action. . . . We did a lot of reading. . . . We were fortunate in that on the high school level, we studied classics. We had classics, which I think today are being given at the college level—very intensive."

Blanche's mother was "an unusual person. She had a lust for life. She was a sick person, she had a heart condition, but she got up in the morning and she'd say, 'Isn't it a gorgeous day!' It was a philosophy of hers." In addition to teaching, Mr. Aronin owned a store in front of their home; he stocked general merchandise. Mrs. Aronin maintained the store.

"My father visited the farmers to buy . . . the materials . . . but she was the one who initiated the store . . . it was really my mother's business. What happened, we had one of these old frame homes and . . . it was [divided]. The front of it was made into a store, so that she was home, you see. [When] we were all growing up . . . everybody helped in making beds, in cooking. . . . So we had good guidance in those early years, and it was a struggle, but we didn't feel we were underprivileged."

When asked by her granddaughter how it was when she was young, Blanche had responded, "When we were young I rode in a horse and sleigh.... We had clothes [that] we'd boil ... on top of a stove. We had a wringer; we hung them up and they froze. We had an outdoor privy for a long time, so we'd bring kerosene lamps [with us]. My granddaughter said, 'Weren't you lucky.' I thought, 'Gee, yes, I think we were lucky.... The distractions today are horrendous."

While Blanche's home situation was a happy, secure one, "My early years weren't [always] happy ones, because I was very much alone.... We were the only Jewish family in Sturgeon Bay. My younger brothers and sisters found peers at the school and other outlets, where I could not. And so that's why I was introspective.... I recall, during the summer my parents would send me to a large city. They were concerned because I was Jewish and had no friends. I wasn't permitted to make many friends, so I remember one summer when I went to Sheboygan and stayed with my grandfather. He would look like Moses, he really did ... [and] the several walls of his rooms [were lined] with books. I was impressed. And at night I heard sounds of him singing; I looked out. He was singing to me downstairs.... He was very understanding, very sensitive—great sense of humor. We respected him."

When Blanche decided to enter the law profession, support and encouragement came from many sources. "Because I was on the debating team and also because my teachers encouraged me to think in terms of law, I progressed to that.... I just wanted to get away from the obvious professions of teacher, librarian, etc.... My teachers in high school were wonderful, particularly one, Miss Reynolds.... She was my English teacher and because I was reading so much, she would keep me after class and we talked about it [the law profession]. She knew I was on the debating team. I think I was the only girl on the debating team, and she said, 'Fine—let's discuss it.' So we did and she encouraged me."

Though her youngest two sisters and a brother were not interested in things academic, Blanche's brother Ben, who was two years younger than she, actively studied Jewish law with her and her father. He "attended Kent College of Law two years after I did. He was a brilliant man, known nationally for his writings, teaching ... [and interpretations of scripture]." A steady influence on his sister's career, "He didn't like the practice of law and after three years of disillusionment, went back to Jewish education.... He had one of [the early Jewish] educational camps in Eagle River [Wisconsin], and . . . for relaxation, he'd get up at six to study Chinese. . . . His mind was fantastic."

Asked if she felt in any way "unusual" as a woman wanting to go to law school, Blanche responded, "I didn't, but everyone else did. . . . It was amazing. Neighbors had come to . . . [my parents] and tried to persuade them not to let their daughter go into law. 'She'll never get anywhere with it. Wouldn't it be better to have a safe career?' But they said, 'If this is what Blanche wants to do, that's all right with us.' "

Blanche's entrance into Chicago-Kent in 1919 preceded the use of the case method there. The method of instruction was "text, lecture, a great deal of lecture; the fact that you don't have to know the law, if you know where to find it—that type of thing. . . . I was used to study. [My high school education] really prepared me for any of what I might have." At that time the school was located in an office at 116 North Michigan. Blanche remembers a "very large room," seating perhaps one hundred students, the professor lecturing from the front of the room. According to Blanche, many of the students did not take law school seriously. "They didn't know why they were studying law. . . . My fellow students wouldn't take me seriously. I had two friends, both of them boys—they were in my class. I was working with them part time so they knew me and that was really the basis of the friendship at least. But otherwise, I'd sit with my book and study, give an occasional answer, but they didn't pay any attention to me. They probably just, shall we say [thought it was] an experiment—that I wasn't going to finish."

The professors, however, "were very nice, treated me the same, no difficulty there. . . . I think they were glad to have women in class." Noting that the professors never discussed what the women were going to do with their law degrees, Blanche asserted, "We were sort of an oddity—just came in and went out. . . . I never felt any [disrespect] as far as they were concerned. Except that I still think they had a feeling that I would never really practice. I think they may have had that in the back of their mind."

Blanche remembers two role models particularly well. The first was a practicing woman lawyer. "In Chicago at that time there was a woman by the name of Pearl Hart. She was an image! She was six feet tall, [with] a masculine haircut. She dressed in men's clothes. She was a wonderful attorney for civil rights. That was [my] image of the lawyer. . . . She was a very strong and vibrant person and she'd appear and get a lot of publicity."

In Blanche's class, "there was one other woman, Agnes Clohesy"—a schoolteacher. "For myself at 17 or 18 . . . oh, she looked very old. I don't think she could have been more than 35 or 40, but to me she seemed to be [old]." She was one of the few students who took school seriously, because she was older, and "this was going to be her vocation."

"I was impressed that there were . . . many black men [studying at night] there, who were working hard to gain this advantageous career. I was impressed by that. And I figured they were doing physical work, many of them had families, and still were giving the time. It was very commendable."

Blanche did belong to the Kappa Beta Pi sorority, but "it didn't mean very much . . . because it was small. We didn't even meet . . . we had four people on the staff. The men had fraternities, so we had to have a sorority. . . . At that time, there was no great discussion about women in a category—women's lib—there was nothing. We went there to study law. It was a healthier attitude, I think, in some respects."

After graduation and passing the bar in 1922, Blanche received considerable attention not only by being a woman lawyer but for being the "youngest ever" female member of the bar. Opportunities, however, were limited; Blanche remained with the law firm that had employed her as a stenographer during her legal education. "It was a good arrangement because I couldn't get a position. Nobody was employing women attorneys. They would always ask, 'Could you also do stenography?' So I did that [remained with the firm]. I had the option of having cases come into the office if I wished. My cases were few and far between. I had some collections, I had a small personal injuries. I had one divorce case, but nothing that would make it possible for me to go on financially unless I was employed."

Two years after graduation, Blanche married, "and then of course we had the two children so I didn't do much of anything at that time. . . . My husband didn't want me to work and at that time women didn't, so I just didn't. I was sorry I didn't. . . . [My husband] had a wholesale dress manufacturing place . . . and we were getting settled, and then we had one baby and then we had another. So that kept me busy. But when they were about 6 or 7 years old I was bored to death. . . . I still tried to get an opening, but I could not unless I could also do stenographic work."

Household circumstances coupled with the Depression propelled Blanche into volunteer work. "I could not possibly just be at home continuously with the children. We had help, a French girl, and so I decided to do volunteer work. . . . People discouraged me from [hanging out my shingle] because where would I get clients? In the first place, people were hesitant about going to women. . . . So then every week I would go and do volunteer work. . . . I didn't really try to get a job as such. I considered myself a volunteer."

This volunteer work began with the Women's League for Conservative Judaism and culminated in an active professional position with this group. "I was attracted to this cultural activity. Later I became the president and then I became the president of the branch—the area which encompasses all Wisconsin and Michigan. [As branch president,] I could introduce social action, politics and other things. [I] stayed with [that] one religious organization. . . . Though people had asked me to come to work for them because I was an organization person and had reorganized a branch, . . . I couldn't. I didn't believe in scattering energy all over the place. I wanted to know this religious practice in depth. This was rewarding, because later, when there was a need to work professionally, I became national coordinator for this organization, which numbered some two hundred thousand women, eight hundred sisterhoods.

"So this was a very good entree to me and the organizational skills which I had developed had been very helpful. . . . I could always go back to stenography but I didn't want to. I felt here I had some chance of motivating people, of enlarging my own dimensions. . . . Very few women with young children were working. . . . Most groups are only interested in you as a person. This group was interested in you as a family. . . ." Blanche and her organization did a great deal of volunteer work with Jewish immigrants who were fleeing Europe during World War II.

"Through the years I have done some legal work. Usually those [cases] which would not require court attendance. People came to me—friends—for help; others have said, 'Would you take this personal injury case?' I remember one case where a black woman came to me—she couldn't get another attorney to handle her personal injury case. I took care of it. Now these cases could be settled out of court today. I took collection cases." Blanche worked out of her home in Rogers Park on the north side of Chicago.

At the start of her sporadic legal career, Blanche recalled being disadvantaged by her lack of practical training at law school and by her inferior position with the law firm for which she worked. "When they gave me something to do, I had to ask. And find my way around. 'And what do you do in this court? And what do you do here?' When I did appear in court, I remember one instance where the judge looked at me and he almost laughed. He sees this small young person coming there, discussing something. . . . I was very hurt, and I never returned to that courtroom."

Despite the insecure position she found in a profession which she had entered with all the enthusiasm of the '20's, Blanche Lippitz was quite glad she had become a lawyer. "It has made me very aware and sensitive to what's going on—Civil Rights, the NOW movement, ... [fighting] the Moral Majority. ... It has made me ... intensely supportive of what this country has. ... I think it is a good system [despite the] corruption. [Though] my brother couldn't take law too long, he did try one very famous case as a young man and was able to save [someone] from the [electric] chair.

"You have to have some background [in law] to understand the current political and sociological scene. ... Because of the ERA, it's been terribly frustrating in Illinois. Illinois should have been divided into two states. The southern part should have joined the south ... long ago. When I went down to Springfield [lobbying for ERA], there were people there I had nothing in common with.

"We were trying to reach the Senators and Congressmen, and I heard a man saying, 'Well, you know if we pass that bill of rights, that means gays will be able to marry.' I thought my hair would stand on end. ... But, as I say, [law] helped me to understand and fight for what I feel—equal rights, as we need them and this country needs them."

But Blanche Lippitz had used law more for background in her religious and political activism than as a career in itself. This she attributed to the lack of opportunity for her when she tried to practice. However, "I don't have to be concerned about women any more. ... They've become members of firms, they get jobs in civic law, municipal jobs, in politics. ... Law is most permissive [for women today]. ... The last few years [have seen] an open door for women [because of] a good economic situation today."

As she spoke, Blanche Aronin Lippitz must have been aware that the economy was slipping once again. Still, the early '80's were "good times" compared to the Depression. Blanche Lippitz did not, to be sure, go on to speculate upon what truly bad times, if they came again, would mean for career women. However, her life story, as well as the others recounted here, provides us with a solid basis for prediction. It is to these predictions, that we will turn in the concluding chapter. First, however, we look at how Chicago women, trained after Blanche Lippitz, tackled law careers in an era stripped of the hopeful illusions of the 1920's.

Edna Cronin Smith: Helpmate in a Male World

In 1914, at the age of 10, Edna Cronin (pseudonym) came to Chicago from Alabama by way of Atlanta.[42] While her father and older brother stayed in Alabama, her mother came north to work as a milliner, bringing Edna and her older sister. The couple was never reconciled, and Edna's mother married again in 1917. Edna's brother soon rejoined the other children but she never saw her real father again. However, her stepfather was to become an important influence in her life.

Edna's stepfather had been a prosecutor in Anderson, Indiana, "and he had law books all around.... I guess that's where I got the idea.... But he didn't keep up with the law and went into the newspaper business. He was the night editor and assistant managing editor of the *Chicago Tribune* for many years, until he retired."

The summer that she graduated from high school, Edna, through her father, got a job in the U.S. Marshall's office in Chicago. While there, she changed her plans to go to Northwestern or the University of Chicago and went instead to night law school at Chicago-Kent. Though her father had been willing to pay for her college, working as a secretary to the Deputy U.S. Marshall gave Edna a measure of independence. While in law school, she switched jobs to become a secretary for a real-estate firm.

Edna's classes at Kent were taught largely by the Socratic method, reflecting a considerably earlier transition to that mode of instruction than occurred at WCL. Her stepfather practiced the give and take of the law with her at home.

The law school itself had just moved to 10 North Franklin, "an old rat trap." The building was "small, very small. There were only two classrooms on a floor. And down on the first floor was the dean's office and the secretary to the dean." There was no library.

Edna was living with her parents. "I worked until 5:00, grabbed a bite to eat, and went over to classes from 6 to 8:30, five nights a week. I studied on weekends; there was not much social life." Apparently, Kent's attempt to give students a part-time law degree in three years by holding classes every weeknight provided very little time for studying, either.

Professor Monahan, who taught criminal law, stood out in Edna's memory: "When we came to crimes against women ... we [women] asked the professor if we could have the night off. The women didn't want to be in the same room, in those days. So the professor said, 'All right.' " Monahan, however, reneged on his promise and not only had the women attend class, but called on them. "We were really embarrassed.... We thought we had been cheated." As a rule, however, Monahan did not pick on women—"just that one trick.... He figured we could learn it so he decided to have it anyhow." The "honor" for "picking on women" fell to Judge Pickett.

Edna and the other students had very little contact with the teachers outside of class. "Everybody was anxious to get home." She did manage some contact with other women students through membership in Kappa Beta Pi. Most women joined this organization; however, "there were only a few [women] in our class," and some of them didn't finish. "There were only five of us in our immediate class at graduation."

Edna still belonged to the sorority after graduation and stayed in touch that way with many of her sisters. But "after graduation the thing to do was to join the Women's Bar Association. After that, the sorority sort of fell into the background. We all joined [the WBA]." Neither the sorority nor the WBA took any political role in the advancement of women "in those days." From what follows, it is also apparent that these organizations were of little use to Edna in her work.

Aside from Judge Pickett, Edna felt she was treated well by her male teachers and classmates. For example, she recalls no comments to her face about her just being there to "catch a husband." But one thing changed while Edna Cronin was attending Kent that would ultimately decrease the number of women in the school—a change in pre-law school requirements by both the bar and the law school.

"In 1923 [the year Edna entered], you could graduate from school and go immediately to college. Then the next year you had to have one year of college. Then . . . two years. They staggered it." By contrast, Boston and Washington, D.C., finally began to require two years of college some ten to fifteen years later. Because of the change in requirements, Kent instituted a junior college in 1924, much as Portia would some eleven years later. As recounted previously, the junior college experiment was dropped after a year, when Kent found it had ample students to fill its classes anyway.

In 1926 Edna Cronin graduated in the top one-third of her class, and took the written bar exam. The next hurdle was a "committee on character and fitness . . . and all that. So when the time came for my appointment . . . [I was young] and there was this long table with all these men sitting around there. And they jumped at you right away with all these questions. I froze. Couldn't even answer the questions. . . . So they postponed it to another date and I was prepared then. I knew what I was going to walk into and so I was all right."

All five of the women who finished school with the class of 1926 took the bar exam. Though Edna passed, her good friend Marion Bird Biderman did not, despite two tries. "She [had been] secretary of the first and third year [classes]. She married in the last year of law

school. . . . I think I'm the only one [of the five women] that went on to use the law."

Passing the bar, however, did not affect the kind of work Edna was doing for the real-estate firm. She did not appear in court, and continued drawing deeds and contracts and "all that you have to do in a real estate office." She married a Mr. Smith (pseudonym) in 1929. The future looked bright.

Then the Depression hit: "This real-estate firm almost went under. After having . . . over one hundred, almost two hundred employees, it went down to about five. . . . We had a law firm representing us . . . and two of the lawyers from this firm used to come over, and of course being in the legal department, I got to know them. . . . So when the [real-estate] firm folded, they asked me to come over with them [in 1932]. . . . But while I was with this law firm, I did nothing but secretarial work. . . . In those days if a woman [was lucky enough to be] on the letterhead of a law firm, she was at the bottom. No, they did not like women practicing law in those days."

In 1935, one of the two lawyers who had brought Edna into the firm left for another office, and Edna went too. "And I stayed there. Well, I went into court a couple of times there. This gentleman had me admitted to practice law in the federal court." But "they" still wouldn't call Edna Cronin Smith a lawyer. "Then I retired in 1937 and stayed home for ten years." The 1930's were a time, it should be remembered, when married women were discouraged from working by prevailing cultural attitudes.

When Edna went back to work in 1947 it was with a "three-man" law firm; she was the third man's secretary. "I really did more legal work there, but I [was never a lawyer]. . . . When they would talk on the phone with somebody, they'd say, 'My associate, Edna Smith' . . . [but that was about it]. No, they just didn't like women in law."

"The women who were practicing were women who didn't get married and . . . were going to make a career out of it. I didn't intend to make a career out of it, really. . . . After having been retired for ten years, I was going back temporarily, and [then] my husband passed away [in 1955].

"And so I just kept on. If I had intended earlier to make it really a big career, I would have . . . you know, really done something. . . . But, [when] you're married, you have your husband, your husband takes care of you. . . . So you don't—it was sort of a temporary thing with me. . . . I think men just thought women were inferior. They felt women just weren't up to it, that's all."

"[There were] no women's law firms. They practiced individually.

We had one . . . Ellen Cerese—[who was] quite prominent here in Chicago. She married a gentleman from Honeywell Corporation, but it didn't last. But she was well known. Then there was . . . a great big lady . . . Pearl Hart. . . . She was more prominent than . . . any woman in Chicago. And she practiced law. But she was alone!"

"We had only one woman judge that I recall . . . Judge Bartelme . . . in the juvenile division. . . . Women just didn't get anywhere in those days like they do today. [Today,] we have a woman on the Supreme Court!"

Edna Cronin Smith was Irish, but the political prominence of her people, apparently did nothing to help her career. She just didn't know the politicians. "In those days, Chicago was divided into ethnic groups. You either lived in the Italian neighborhood, the Irish neighborhood, the black neighborhood, or the Jewish neighborhood," and rarely did the different groups meet. "You married someone from your own neighborhood."

Edna's neighborhood had been on the West Side of Chicago, north of 12th Street. "The Jewish community was on the West Side, south of 12th Street . . . and you didn't overstep. Then the Jewish people started coming north of 12th Street . . . and the Irish all moved out. [Then] the Jewish people moved out and the Italians moved in. [Finally,] the Italians moved out and the blacks are in."

If her ethnicity didn't help, Edna felt her lack of a college education before law school was an active hindrance. "I think I would have had a broader perspective if I had had [it]. . . . Going right from high school to law school—there seems to be a lapse in there somehow."

Attending a night law school was also a barrier, despite Edna's good grades. "In those days employers didn't inquire into [your class standing] if you went to a part-time school." However, if you went to the University of Chicago "and belonged to the Order of the Coif [an honor society], things were different. Other than that, nobody cared."

Edna was never told that she stood in the top third of her class and never asked. "I thought I barely made it through." In retrospect, "I [wonder] if I would have done better if I had gone into teaching. . . . That would have been traditional [for women]–and the marvelous pensions they get when they quit!" Edna, of course, got no pension from her own jobs.

However, teachers "didn't have such a good time of it during the Depression. . . . The teachers got warrants. They weren't paid, you know. . . . So they'd sell the warrants to somebody and get what they could [for them]. . . . And I worked during the Depression and got paid." Occasionally, she had also been able to write a will for a friend, and make a little extra "on the side."

"When I was working, I talked to a girl who asked me [for advice] about becoming a lawyer, and [I told her] to think it over very, very carefully. [Although] women are coming more to the fore all the time, I don't really think they've reached the pinnacle yet where men can say they'd consider them equal . . . that is, taking them in as law partners and so on."

It seemed a "plus" to Edna, however, that many women are now getting legal education and entry-level jobs. "When I went to law school, . . . most of those people in that class [men or women] never practiced law. They did it just to have the knowledge in their business or profession. . . . Out of our class, [we had] three judges here in Chicago, and one state's attorney. I guess that's about all the prominent people that came out of our class." None of these "prominent" people, of course, were women; and few of the women had a significant "business or profession" to fall back on.

World War II had little effect on women lawyers' chances, as far as Edna Cronin Smith could tell. What the war did, however, was break up the old ethnically-centered neighborhood system. Before the war "if you lived in Chicago, you would marry someone from Chicago and oftentimes from the same neighborhood . . . [but when] the boys were sent to different states in the service . . . [they] met girls in other states and other places. They would [often] go live where the wife was reared. . . . And so it changed."

But the war and all its changes passed by, with Edna Cronin Smith, member of the bar, tending a childless home. Hers is a poignant story, told with a certain regret. Had she already given up, before changes in mobility began to open new opportunities? One could hardly blame her, given the bleakness of the prospects presented by a society in Depression. Men such as those "at the long table," who made her "freeze" at the bar exam, had controlled her much of her life; yet she had served them and served them well. In the circumstances, it would have taken a giant of a personality to do much more.

Sabra Stein: Night School Lawyer

Clearly, the optimism Chicago-Kent women like Blanche Aronin carried with them to law school was muted by the harsh reality of the 1930's. Whereas Blanche was sheltered from much of this disappointment by her marriage to a successful man and her concentration on family, Edna Cronin Smith's attempts to gain full status as a lawyer were continually thwarted. The lack of women in Chicago-Kent classes in the 1930's mirrored the realities of the time. Instead of building their numbers from the five graduating with Edna Cronin Smith, only one or two women per class graduated from Kent in the late '30's.

When Sabra Stein (pseudonym) graduated from Kent in 1938, she was the only woman in her class.[43] By that time Kent's founding chapter of Kappa Beta Pi, begun with such high hopes, "practically didn't exist." Although graduating with high honors and Law Review status, all Sabra could do was to continue as a legal secretary for the large and prestigious "Sonnenschein firm" (Now Sonnenschein, Nathan and Carl). She soon realized that the only way she might get out of her secretarial niche was by working for the government, particularly in Washington, D.C.

In 1940 Sabra Stein took Civil Service exams both for the position of lawyer and for the "Clerical, Administrative and Fiscal" rating. "And I thought, well, if I get a job in Washington as a clerk, or a secretary . . . I'll go around from agency to agency until I get a job as a lawyer." Though she got a quasi-legal clerical job, she did not become a lawyer. When offered a job back in Illinois, as unemployment compensation deputy, she quickly took it.

Sabra was married to another "night school lawyer" who had been unable, despite his first-in-the-class ranking at DePaul, to move beyond docket clerk at the Sonnenschein firm. "The lawyers at Sonnenschein were Harvard, Michigan graduates—all that kind of thing. So naturally they looked down on [us]. One of [them] said to me: 'What law school are you [from]?' And I said: 'Kent.' . . . He shook his head—[and made] a terrific pun: 'Kent—Kent learn anything!' "

Although Sabra's husband eventually made a good living as a lawyer, Sabra herself turned to bearing and raising their four children after the war. Faced with a number of obstacles—she was a night school graduate, female, Jewish, and married—she put considerable emphasis on the night school stigma. "[If I had it to do again,] I would try to go to a day school." She doubted that the big firms of her day (of which only a few were Jewish and thus theoretically open to her) hired night school graduates as lawyers. What is more, "they weren't hiring women at all." What she saw as a situation in the private bar had caused her to apply to the federal government. "I can't tell you how many women lawyers I met in Washington." Once settled in Chicago raising a family, Washington was no longer a possibility. After her children were grown, and no doubt remembering her exclusion from Chicago's private bar, she finished her career as an editor for the Commerce Clearing House—a publisher of practitioners' guides.

Still, the 1930's did provide avenues into the private bar for realistic women lawyers with no dreams of practicing in big firms on LaSalle Street. Our interviews conclude with the stories of two such women—Liberty Petru Dvorak, who practiced with male family members—and Edith Renier Johnson, who "went it alone."

Liberty Petru Dvorak: A Family Practice

Liberty Petru Dvorak's story is typical of the 1930's dual-career family.[44] As wife and, later, mother practicing law, Liberty became adept at switching roles as the situation warranted. The primacy she placed on family at first necessitated a helpmate role in practice with her attorney husband.

Born the youngest of three children in a family that had emigrated from Czechoslovakia, Liberty Bond Petru grew up in an atmosphere that encouraged education. Her father graduated not only from high school, but also from business college, after which he entered the real-estate profession. Liberty's sister graduated from the University of Illinois and was in her first year of medical school when she decided to marry instead. Her brother went on to become a lawyer and was to have an influential role in Liberty's own decision to do so.

While education seemed to be a central force in the Petru family, Liberty was not under any sort of pressure to "become" anything. "From the time I was little, I'd go down to my Dad's office with him and sort of do things around there. . . . At that time the real-estate men and the lawyers worked together on [transactions]. . . and I just sort of got into the business end of it. When I said I was going to be a lawyer, they all wondered, but saw me through." When asked about her parents' reactions to her going to law school, Liberty responded, "They were surprised when I finished—that I didn't get married before [that]! They let us decide what we wanted. . . . By being a woman maybe I should [have been] surprised but I don't know, they didn't feel that way. They were glad I was going into, and studying, something that I liked."

Before she entered law school, Liberty attended the University of Illinois to meet the Illinois bar requirements of two years prelegal education, and majored in commerce. It was participation in "outside activities at the college . . . like [student] government . . . that [provided] the background for law." Although she would not have been kept out of any of the Chicago area law schools on grounds of sex ("There was no problem as far as the women were concerned"), Liberty chose Chicago-Kent because of the relative ease of commuting from her home in Cicero. "At the time people liked going into the city law schools. I had a lot of judges as my teachers.... They said, 'You're learning the practical end ... of law.' "

At Chicago-Kent "I was [often] the only girl in the class, ... a reflection of the reality of the Depression for women. In some of them there were two of us, or sometimes three but that's about all.... It didn't bother me.... [The University of] Illinois was so big ... you were just one of many ... and never felt [like an] individual. Maybe if I had gone to a small school and there [were] a lot of girls around me, I'd have felt a little bit different" at Kent.

With a lawyer/older brother to coach her, Liberty did not find law school particularly surprising. She knew she would be taught by the case method and "get called on plenty.... As long as I was prepared it didn't make me nervous!" As a day student, "I did have smaller classes.... It was a very warm school.... I'd come down early and study at the library. We did have a nice, I mean a nice, library for that size of a school." After a morning of studying, Liberty would have lunch and attend the afternoon session.

The only social activity Liberty found time to take part in was Alpha (founding) chapter of Kappa Beta Pi legal sorority. "They wanted to promote women, that was the idea, not the ERA-type deal. It was promoting women to go into law, for higher education, professional education.... Why the sorority held together is that even after you graduated you were still active members of the Alpha chapter. It was only of late that we decided to have the professional group so we could mix with others in other law schools." Though such networking via the sorority might have helped her had it been employed as in Washington, apparently women in the Chicago bar lacked sufficient numbers and influence to make this happen.

As for the teachers' treatment of her, "I think at times maybe one or two would think, 'Let's see what she's going to do here, is she going to stay, going to study?'.... I would say that they took us just as one of the boys. They weren't going to mark you out just because you were a woman. On the same token, you had to be that way too. You couldn't [say], 'Well, because I'm a woman you have to treat me differently.' "

While some women thought they got called on in class more than the men, Liberty "never thought that way. There's a little bit of cooperation you had to give. Well, you had to cooperate with the teacher as much [as] you would [cooperation] like yourself. As a fellow would too. I never realized that they called on me more; maybe they did. I don't know. I wasn't watching for it."

Graduating in June of 1939, Liberty married her brother's law partner, a Mr. Dvorak, and started working for them "in the middle of 1940. I didn't 'join,' I just was working for them at first, but then the war came around and my brother had to go in because he had a commission. And my husband went in, so I was left with the firm." Originally, "I thought I might work for the state's attorney's office.... They offered me a pretty good job.... [But] my brother and husband thought they better keep me because of the war situation." So Liberty took over the practice. "[But] I always thought, for a woman that would be [the only way to do it.] Luckily I had someone to step in with. But to go out on my own—no, I never planned to do that."

Liberty observed, "In comparing [the legal profession then] to today, it was harder for the women to get in. I don't know if it was just because they were women, or just the fact that the men [discriminated] or the places just weren't open as they are today; you have a lot more government offices open today." Two major employers of women attorneys at that time were Commerce Clearing House and the Railroad Retirement Board. For example, Sabra Stein, who was at Kent during Liberty's years, ended up working for the former. "Of course you had to start in at low pitch. And then if you were good enough you worked yourself up. But now when you get out of law school there isn't that problem.... If they have places and they're open, you get in."

Once back from the war, Liberty's brother retired and moved to California, which meant that Liberty and her husband were now law partners. In 1947, Liberty's only child, a son, was born. "I was fortunate to get good help, but I still only [worked] part-time then.... I practiced a little bit from my home along with the part-time work. But when he went to high school,... originally it was two days, three days, then I probably expanded to four days. But I still wanted to give him [time] being a mother at home and doing things with him. I think for a woman I was fortunate.... I was able to be flexible with my time. If I couldn't handle something, my husband would handle it for me.... I don't think [law is] the best career for a woman who's going to get married. In other fields, such as nursing or teaching, you can always get part-time work without any problem. [With] law work, you're either in it or you are out.... The thing is, if I wasn't pushed [by] this war into it, I probably wouldn't have gotten as involved [in the legal profession] as I did."

Liberty kept in touch with the school and the sorority, and became active in the Women's Bar Association of Illinois. "Originally it was the most wonderful thing to join because it got all the women together. . . . I got to know all of them." At that time the Women's Bar was a small organization and unlike today, was largely social rather than political. "But now of course, there is no problem at all. [Women] get pretty good appointments. And I will say the Women's Bar does back them.

"I've been asked to talk to some young girls who wanted to go into law. I always say, 'Go ahead.' Because for me it was an experience, and everybody needs some type of experience." But now that law students need four years of college prelegal education, "I tell these girls, be sure to take enough courses to teach or something, so that you can go back and just take a year of something and get another profession without any problem." These were not her only words of caution.

Liberty's son had gone through Kent as well and is now practicing in the same building in which his mother and father worked. Asked what additional advice she would have given him had he been female, Liberty responded: "[Don't] believe that when you get through law school you're going to take the world by the horns and just throw it around. I mean you've got to plug a little bit. . . . Girls coming out now [are] getting this . . . getting that. . . . It's [no longer] a struggle, but you have to work at it. In other words, if you get a job and you have to type a little bit or something, [don't say,] 'I'm not for that, that's not my work; I'm an attorney.' A lot of men attorneys type. . . . You get to do a little underground as well as overground work is the way I put it. . . . In other words, don't be too big."

One senses in these words both an envy of the greater entry opportunities of current women lawyers and an attempt to warn them that their opportunities may not prove as great as they now seem. While current feminists may be justified in warning women *not* to type when they get into a law office, one wonders what the best choice will be if the job situation gets really desperate and women lawyers have not yet gained significant control over the profession. In any event, Liberty appears to be correct in warning today's women against overconfidence.

Despite the hardships, Liberty never disliked being a lawyer. "I've met a lot of fine people and I must say I've never really met a man who has been anything but a gentleman to me while I practiced law. . . . [However,] you had to act like a man when you [were] practicing law . . . in my time. . . . [But never say,] 'You can't do this to me—

I'm a woman'.... Many times I would laugh about it, because there [was] a man who said, 'Oh, don't tell me it's a woman attorney!' You had to take chances like a man did, you couldn't be picky. So I enjoyed my work."

Liberty Dvorak did what society required of her and practiced law too.

Edith Renier Johnson: The Triumph of Personality over Disability

Personality could overcome even the insecurity engendered in women lawyers by the cultural attitudes of the 1930's. Partially deaf from an early age, Edith Renier '39 refused to let this physical handicap deter her; in fact her resolve seems to have been strengthened because of it.[45]

Born in Chicago and educated in the public school system, Edith first became fully aware of her handicap in eighth grade: "I had a teacher who discovered I wasn't hearing.... I had a history book opened and she was teaching geography. I didn't even know what she was teaching. She said to me, The fact that you're hard of hearing is not your fault, but your attitude is'.... My teacher's attitude taught me that when I got in a situation where I realized I wasn't hearing, I stopped them immediately and I told them I couldn't hear and had this handicap. And I do that to judges even."

If this teacher must be given some credit for Edith's forthrightness, Edith's mother may have been the root cause of her fierce determination. "My mother never let me use the word 'can't.' Whenever I said I couldn't do something, she asked me if I had tried.... When I was very young my mother made me memorize poetry." Edith then recited the poetry at various "lodges" in front of adults.

This early training perhaps explains Edith's "comeback" after suffering a heart attack between the ages of 12 and 13. Despite being forced to sit out a year of school, she nevertheless entered high school, made the honor society, caught up on her credits and managed to graduate in three years. At this point in her life, Edith's parents "didn't believe that a girl needed an education ... and they opposed my going to school. When I graduated from high school there was no question of my going to college. My mother's reaction to me was 'Well, who would go to a woman lawyer?' They didn't realize I would make a success. So all the more reason I was determined."

Her parents' own educational background may have contributed to this opposition to further education for Edith; in her own words, they were "self-taught." Her mother graduated from grammar school, "worked until she was 17 years old, then she married my father." Her father "was born in Germany and came here when he was 6. He was one of twelve children. . . . My father only went to third grade, and then his father made him go to work. He was a pattern cutter of ladies' dresses." The strongest influence came from her brother, ten years her senior and a graduate of Chicago-Kent College of Law, who "induced me to study law."

This inducement came after Edith was turned away from normal school (teacher's college). "My secret ambition was to teach maladjusted boys, not deficient, not mentally deficient boys, but boys who were off on the wrong track. I was told I had an aptitude for this . . . and I passed the written examination, but did not pass the oral. . . . The dean called me into his office and said, 'I'm not to be quoted, but you don't have the right political connections.' I announced to my parents that I didn't have the right political connections [to obtain a seat in the Chicago Teacher's College during the Depression]. An uncle wanted me to see a Charlie Weber, who was an alderman in Chicago, [but] I said I'd sweep floors before I became beholden to him.

"My brother said, 'I'm glad you didn't make it, because you'd make a better lawyer.' While he was in law school he [would] give me hypothetical cases and ask me what I would do with them. And then I would answer him and he'd say: 'Well, any monkey can come to a conclusion, but what is your reasoning?' And so he decided for me that that was the way to go." About this time, her father came to like the idea of two of his children as lawyers, and permitted Edith to live at home and work her way through law school, though she had to pay room and board.

Conveniently, Edith worked in the office of the law school, and attended classes at night. Often she would work until 6:25 to make extra money and then dash upstairs for a 6:30 class, just in time to answer "here" when roll was called. Studying occupied every spare moment—in the lunchroom, on the daily commute via the "el," and during the entire weekend. In part this was due to what seemed to be a higher standard for the women: "In most of the classes I was the only girl. Occasionally there would be one or two others, but it seemed like they would come and go. They didn't stay. I guess they felt [that the teachers] made it hard for them . . . that the instructors made it difficult. But I felt the instructors were really doing me a favor, and old Judge Pickett would call on me every single day, which meant I had to be prepared. . . . So it was great discipline. In a way he was doing me a favor. But he would sit at a desk and he'd lean over with his bushy eyebrows and he'd say, 'Now, what does the young lady have to say about this?' And I felt like it was a big dog coming down."

Singling Edith out for attention may have had the opposite effect of that intended—it spurred her to excel rather than frightening her away. Apparently Judge Pickett wasn't the only teacher to call on women more than on the men. "In not all [courses], but some of them, I knew I'd be called on. . . . It didn't bother me . . . it made me study."

And yet, "I never had the feeling that they were picking on me. It's just that, I think that, first of all, . . . I weighed about 99 pounds and I looked younger than I was and I didn't have any clothes, and made my clothes out of my mother's dresses. . . . So I think they took one look at me and figured that I wasn't [good] material. They were going to just smoke it out and see. And if I wasn't good material, then weed me out."

"The school itself was a narrow building, three stories high, and the classrooms had wooden chairs [with an armrest]. The professors were on a platform, which made it more difficult for me to hear, because of being hard of hearing—the voices went up. I would sit in the front row and I generally put my feet up on the platform and braced my books. I got a lot of my knowledge from the printed page and [by] eye, more than I did from what I heard."

Heeding her eighth grade teacher's advice, Edith told all her law teachers about her deafness. "I could tell by the way they looked at me that they were calling on me, and if I didn't understand the question, I didn't hesitate to ask them." One can picture Edith Renier, hearing poorly, a woman alone in a large, drab classroom, with fifty male classmates.

Edith was too poor to join the sorority for some feminine companionship. As for men, "Once in a while . . . the fellows would ask me to go out. . . . I'd look at my clothes and think: 'Doesn't he know this is all I have?' And how could I go to a dance or anything? I didn't have any formals or anything. I couldn't afford them."

The long hours of work and study did not leave Edith much time for a social life, anyway. "I think I did go to some of the sorority meetings . . . when I got more advanced, but it wasn't the main part of my life. And I don't belong to the women's bar either. I just felt like it's a lot of wasted time, and I know I can't solve world affairs and all that sort of thing. I can only do [things] where I am. . . . I don't look for the prestige connected with some of those people." She did develop her contacts in other ways, but only after trying to go it alone.

Edith Renier, despite her isolation, felt well treated by her male classmates. "When I got my license, I went down to Springfield . . . on the train [to be sworn in]. My picture was in the paper, the evening paper, on the way coming home, and someone circled my picture and brought it into the train, and said: 'This is our gal,' ... and they seemed like they were kind of proud of me." Only sixteen other Illinois women got their licenses at the same time Edith did.

Independent and hard-working all through law school, Edith turned down her brother's offer to form a partnership when she got out. Her response, when he asked if it was going to be "Renier and Renier," was, "I want no part of that. I will always be kid sister to you, you would feed it to me with a spoon, and I would be your errand girl. I want to go out and see what I can do on my own." Five years later, Edith refused him again: "No. We're too much alike; you want to be the boss and I want to be the boss." Thus Edith struck out on her own.

But fate was to have a hand in hanging Edith's shingle. Just three days after getting her license to practice law, Edith met the man who subsequently became her husband. "He was running for ward committeeman, and he rang my doorbell. I started discussing politics with him and he said, 'Say, you know quite a bit, I could use you in my organization.' And I said 'Well, I don't know you, maybe if I did I'd work against you.' So he said 'Why don't we get acquainted and find out?' "

For Edith and her future husband, "getting acquainted" took place at political meetings. Finally Edith agreed to take a precinct, and "I got active politically. Naturally I had to canvas the homes in my area and I got acquainted with those [families] and some of those people are still clients of mine.... Then I got elected Secretary of the Ward Organization in the 50 Wards.... And of course as such, I got acquainted with all the correspondence; [knowing] everything gave me a wide range of [contacts].... You have to make contacts."

Edith had a flair for making the best of every opportunity which came her way. "I rented desk space in a real estate office and one of the things I did was make out income tax returns, which was a marvelous contact, because I always gave them a card and they would trust me to make out their income tax, when they might not have trusted [me] with something else. It gave me a chance to get acquainted that way. I really burned the midnight oil doing that."

This arrangement with the real estate firm terminated when Edith discovered the broker was gambling. "He borrowed money from me and he gave me a check that bounced, and I decided not to be connected there, so I had to find another office." She found an office with a contractor who, with his partner, bought vacant lots on which to build. "So I started working for them and I traced . . . [titles] and got as many vacant lots as I could lined up in a block so they could buy them and go in and build. . . . As a result of the connections there, I met other builders and so I started handling a lot of work for new construction companies, representing their side." Once established in private practice, Edith accepted a job handling receiverships. "The State of Illinois had like 489 defunct banks that were all put under the Auditor of Public Accounts, and so I took that job and I helped to liquidate these defunct banks—which was a marvelous experience for me also."

Hard work and dedication to her clients were closely allied with Edith's political route to success as a female attorney. "In the beginning there wasn't anything I would not do. I took everything—divorce cases, you name it. . . . Any case that anybody came in with, I took. . . ." When her brother was operated on, "they severed his spinal cord, and I handled his business and my business for 18 months until he could come back. . . . He was in a wheelchair. . . . Now today I handle a great deal of probate work and incompetence and so on, because my clients are getting up in years." Many of these clients have been hers for nearly forty years.

"If you want to be a success, [remember that] your business depends upon people. I think you have to be genuinely interested in [them]. I think the significant thing with my clientele is how many of them say: 'I feel at ease with you' and 'I trust you.' And I think they feel that when I give them advice I'm doing it because I'm really interested in trying to help them and it's not that I'm promoting my own financial good. That has been my practice."

Apparent too is the respect Edith earned from clerks of court. "Sometimes in the morning I'd have to appear before three different judges; maybe one would be on the ninth, one on the eleventh, and one on the seventh. So I'd try to get one motion up near the top of the call and one down. And then I'd say to the clerk, "Now, if I'm not here, hold my call 'til the end.' And they all worked with me.

"[Once] I got assigned and moved to a new judge that didn't know me. Before I even appeared before him I went to his chambers and said 'Your honor, I don't hear well; I wear a hearing aid, so if you will please keep your voice up, it will save your time and aggravation and mine too.' I only had one hearing aid and everything sounded [sort of far away]. And I wore batteries that weighed two pounds that were strapped to my leg—and [this pack] caused much static in the hearing aid!

"The judges were marvelous to me. And once in a while I would get opposing counsel that thought they were going to take advantage by kind of talking [low and jumbled]. And the judges would lean over and say, 'SPEAK UP! I can't hear you.' And I knew they were doing it for my benefit." Obviously, they admired a woman lawyer who had made her own way in the profession, against even greater odds than most of her counterparts.

*****

The story of Edith Renier Johnson is the last story of the women in law in this book. There are of course many women lawyers today who graduated after 1939, including the mass of new lawyers graduating after 1970. No doubt a book could be written based on the observations of these younger women lawyers; such observations, however, are quite close to the events they describe and have been tempered insufficiently by time. Instead I have chosen to speak with those whose lives span vast changes in American life, and whose wisdom has the virtue of perspective.

In reflecting on the gift these women gave to the strangers who peered into their lives, I am reminded of the need for contact between those who have been and those who seek to become. In each woman's struggle for a full and rewarding life, we might hope to see mirror-images of ourselves. Despite their age, most radiate that strength and hope so characteristic of their sex and their nation. For these were women of all backgrounds, who thrust themselves willingly into the cauldron of American life, testing the limits of their freedom. Through that testing, they expanded both their freedom and our own.

6

Conclusion: As Women First and Lawyers Second

Anyone, but particularly a man, must be cautious in interpreting the foregoing life histories:

> "History as traditionally recorded and interpreted by historians had been . . . in fact, the history of the activities of men ordered by male values . . . [The few women] who have been recorded at all [include those] who have performed roles usually reserved for men."[1]

Although many of those interviewed performed roles "usually reserved for men," it may be inaccurate to view their lives through the prism of masculine attitudes about success and failure.

The lives of these women, which did not include senior positions in government or membership in "Wall Street" law firms, often reveal a richness and fabric that is absent from the lives of "successful" lawyers. Yet, this is not the only point to be made. Though "women have created the supportive infrastructure upon which men have built economic and political institutions which allocate and distribute power"[2] and may, to some extent have been content in doing so, they have not had the *opportunity* to do what men do. Thus, a number of women who would prefer to enter and remain in careers outside the home and local community have been denied this chance. On the other hand, men who have wanted to concentrate more on family and community have generally been welcomed by women and stymied chiefly by the attitudes of their male peers.

Who among women chose to study law in the 1920's and 1930's? The study reveals a clear answer: all kinds. Many lost interest and never completed school; others who did, never became members of the bar. Not becoming licensed to practice was not perceived as a crushing blow by most of these women, particularly in the bleak economic times of the 1930's. To give up a "back up" job (not career) that would pay little or nothing, was no great loss to women like Letitia Paraboschi, concerned as they were with home and family.

Those women who perservered through both law school and bar examination, fell into a number of categories. One pattern, not so common at Portia and WCL, but more so at B.U. and Chicago-Kent, was that of active practice with male family members. Grace Minton O'Hare and Susanne Shallna of B.U., (interviewed, but not discussed) practiced with their husbands, as did Liberty Dvorak of Chicago-Kent, who also practiced with her brother. Jacqueline Lloyd Guild of Portia worked with her attorney father. As Cynthia Epstein reported, half of the women lawyers she studied who were married, were married to male lawyers.[3] Like Sabra Stein of Chicago-Kent, not all practiced with their lawyer husbands. Those who did practice with a family member, of course, gained the flexibility in and out of the profession necessary for a woman also concerned with home and family. Another common pattern was exhibited by Portia graduates Mildred Salerno and Sarah Wallace (until later in life), who concentrated on marriage and family, taking only occasional cases.

Careers allied to law were also common. Of WCL graduates, Maude Pryse in real estate and Jane Collier (pseudonym-interviewed but not discussed) in banking took this route, although Collier, being single, pursued her calling as a career in a fuller sense than did Mrs. Pryse.

Several Washington, D.C. graduates became prominent figures in politics and government. Nadine Gallagher of WCL became a trial judge in D.C., and Marguerite Rawalt of George Washington became not only a top attorney with the Internal Revenue Service, but a national leader in the struggle for women's equality. World War II provided government entry via the military for Elizabeth Denny of WCL (Navy) and Helene Lawrence of Portia (Coast Guard). Both stayed in government service, although not ultimately the military, after the war.

All of the women mentioned above were married, save Jane Collier. This was not the case, however, for those women who wanted a full-time private practice, independent of family. Since no firm would hire them as the equivalent of male attorneys, Janet Morgan (WCL), Gladys Shapiro (Portia) and Charlotte Slavitt (B.U.) painstakingly built their own solo practices, and none of them married. Women graduates of the 1920's and 1930's who were not wealthy could not afford the household help and other support necessary to mix marriage and family with the business and professional demands of such a practice; besides, social attitudes of the time encouraged wives, and particularly mothers, to spend considerable time in the home. By contrast, wealthy women had little financial or social incentive to practice law. Already members of the establishment, they needed only to cement their position by marriage.

For those women lawyers who sought the same career opportunities as men, the experience which began in the thirties must have been a very bitter pill. The reader can sense in those portions of the interviews I have reproduced, that, though time has covered many of the wounds, some are still very deep. Often it is difficult to tell what is post-hoc rationalization of the paths taken and what were the real reasons. The reader will often have to make such decisions by reading between the lines—lines often suggesting a profound ambivalence.

*****

The answer to the question of whether history will repeat itself for women lawyers probably lies with the emerging woman lawyer herself. By sheer weight of numbers, more and more exceptional women are breaking into "power positions," such as senior partnerships, tenured professorships, and important judgeships. One hopes that these women will remember their sisters, and not "pull up the ladder." Networks of women lawyers can help even exceptional women lawyers; they are vital for the advancement of those not so gifted. If the women who "make it," put blinders on to the discrimination that still faces less exceptional women, the women's movement cannot ultimately succeed in the male-dominated professions. Those in a position to help may become so oriented to the male-dictated values of their profession that female networking will fail.[4]

Many of the more successful women lawyers we spoke with, particularly those whose careers were formed outside of Washington, D.C., appear uninterested in women's networks. The same phenomenon was noted in medicine by Dr. Michelle Harrison in her book *A Woman in Residence;* most of her female colleagues adopted male attitudes even toward the practice of obstetrics and gynecology, seeing this as the way to be "accepted" and "to get along" in their profession.[5] Though understandable, this route is not likely to produce the more flexible, open profession that even these women may want to see.

Exceptional professional women must realize that they did not achieve what they have sheerly by dint of their own efforts; the way was paved by women, like those we interviewed, who struggled before them. Since they must ultimately fail in an attempt to become fully "one of the boys," why make such an effort, with its negative implications for the progress of their sisters? Highly successful men rarely ignore the need for interdependence, even if purely for their own self interest. Exceptional women could help themselves and other women by following suit.

Only by disregarding the attractive, but dangerous American notion of absolute self-reliance, can the large female networks necessary for every woman in law to reach her potential be established. This will involve overcoming the American bias toward individualism and suspicion of ideology.[6] Only through such networks can these women adapt the legal profession to the needs of those of the species who bear its children and nurture them as infants. The flexibility of time and workload that most women will require can only be achieved by ridding the profession of its competitive, workaholic, and hierarchical characteristics. This should produce as a byproduct, men increasingly inclined toward, and more able to share, in the burdens of the home.

In the 1920's and 1930's, women lawyers achieved only limited success in networking, and that occurred chiefly in the Washington area. Chapters of Kappa Beta Pi and other legal sororities in the Washington area were able to bring female students together with women who had advanced in the profession, largely by means of the government jobs that had been opened to them during the New Deal. Some of these women then favored the younger women when it came to hiring. However, even the Washington effort was never fully successful. It can be argued that women in law in the 1930's were never present in sufficient numbers to withstand the effects of the Depression, regardless of networking. But this lack of numbers may have itself been contributed to by the ineffectiveness of networking. Since lack of numbers is no longer much of a problem, networking today should fail only if the women already in place allow it to fail.

Emotionally secure men can, of course, help as they have always done. Time and again our interviewees spoke of the helping hand extended by such men. But sufficient numbers of these men do not exist, particularly within the competitive, hierarchical professional structures men themselves have fashioned. Women lawyers today must seize the moment that history has presented them to work as a group to gain access to all levels of the profession.

At the same time that their numbers present them with unprecedented opportunity, an uncertain economy presents women lawyers with a critical problem. Some networking of an informal kind is in place, but formal women's networking has lagged behind, due in large part to women's desire to participate in male-dominated professional organizations. Women still have not made it to the power positions in the profession in sufficient numbers to affect significantly the way the profession is run and the criteria it uses for professional advancement.

Whether or not economic times continue to worsen, women lawyers should act decisively to promote women's networking. Such collective action may be necessary as a tactic, until exceptional women lawyers gain their share of top jobs, and of their less talented sisters acquire the same opportunities as ordinary male lawyers. When women have infiltrated the profession to this degree, it will be natural for their male counterparts to view them as lawyers first and women second.

If and when this day arrives, women will, I am convinced, have improved the profession, moving it away from adversariness toward conciliation; and away from hierarchy and competitiveness toward cooperation. At this point, women can allow the concerns of a changed profession to dominate their lives. They can then turn their attention to building "old colleague" networks, instead of weaving the "old girl" fabric that is now necessary.

Notes

1. INTRODUCTION

1. G. Santayana, 1 *The Life of Reason* 284 (1905).

2. C. Epstein, *Women in Law* 4 Table 1.1 (1981).

3. *See* F.L. Allen, *Only Yesterday* 73-101 (1964).

4. Jacqueline Guild Lloyd, interview with Laurie Applefeld, Summer, 1981, Boston, Mass.

5. J.S. Lemons, *The Woman Citizen* vii, viii (1973).

6. *See id.,* at 5. For a short biography of Alice Paul, *see* 63 *Wom. L.J.* 131 (1971).

7. Stricker, "Cookbooks and Law Books: The Hidden History of Career Women in 20th Century America," in N. Cott & E. Pleck eds., *A Heritage of Her Own* 477 (1979).

8. Lemons, *supra* note 5, at 41.

9. Babson, "Trek of Women into Men's Jobs Gains Apace, Babson Declares," Washington Post, Jan. 9, 1939, at 18, col. 2.

10. Milkman, "Women's Work and the Economic Crisis," Cott & Pleck, *supra* note 7, at 522.

11. Lemons, *supra* note 5, at 3.

12. *See* Milkman, *supra* note 10, at 530.

13. *See* Stricker, *supra* note 7, at 476.

14. *See generally,* M. Harrison, *A Woman in Residence* (1982).

15. Epstein, *supra* note 2, at 35.

16. *See* "Law School Attendance (Figures for 1980)" in American Bar Association, *A Review of Legal Education in the United States: Fall 1980–81: Law Schools and Bar Admission Requirements* 49 (1981).

17. Epstein, *supra* note 2, at 381.

18. *See, e.g.,* "The Golden Anniversary History of *Kappa Beta Pi* Legal Sorority," 42 *Kappa Beta Pi Quarterly* 5 (Dec. 1958).

19. *See* D. McGuigan, *A Dangerous Experiment* which details the history of women at the University of Michigan Law School.

Women at such state full-time schools also faced great difficulties in employment, even in Washington and during the New Deal. J. Auerbach, *Unequal Justice* (1976) recounts at 188 the repeated, unsuccessful efforts of a female law review editor from the University of Wisconsin to get New Deal employment through Justice Felix Frankfurter.

20. Epstein, supra note 2.

21. *See* J. Hoopes, *Oral History* 33 (1982).

22. *Cf. id.* at 85, 93.

23. *Cf. id.* at 119.

24. *Cf. id.* at 139.

2. 1920's & 1930's

1. U.S. Dept. Commerce, *Statistical Abstract of the United States* 416, table 687 (1979).

2. ABA *Membership Statistical Report* (Jan. 1983)

3. Tate, "Women and the Legal Profession" 65 *Wom. L.J.* (Fall, 1979).

4. *Id.*

5. *See generally,* M. Walsh, *Doctors Wanted: No Women Need Apply* (1977).

6. *Id.* at 107–108.

7. P. Hummer, *The Decade of Elusive Promise (1920–1930)* 48 (1976).

8. Walsh, *supra* note 5.

9. *See* Hummer, *supra* note 7 for numbers of law students; for admission to the Bar, see Barnes, 23 *J. Leg. Ed.* 276 (1970).

10. Straus, "The Woman Lawyer," in L. H. Farmer, ed., *What America Owes to Women* 289 (1920). *See* B. Harris, *Beyond Her Sphere: Women and the Professions in American History* 112 (1978).

11. Walsh, supra note 5, at 206.

12. *See* Stevens, "Two Cheers for 1870: The American Law School," in D.R. Nolan ed., *Readings in the History of the American Legal Profession* 224 (1980).

13. Hummer, *supra* note 7, at xvii, 3.

14. *Id.* at 47. For an extended discussion of professionalization, *see* B.J. Bledstein, *The Culture of Professionalism* (1976).

15. This occurred despite the efforts of Elihu Root, chairman of a special ABA committee, to discredit the recommendation of Alfred Z. Reed, for the Carnegie Foundation, that such schools be retained. *See generally* J. Auerbach, *Unequal Justice* 102–129 (1976).

16. Hummer, *supra* note 7, at 70.

17. C. Epstein, *Women in Law* 5 (1981).

18. Robbins, "Opportunity's Haven: The Ambiguous Heritage of Suffolk University Law School," *The Advocate (Suffolk Law School): 75th Anniversary Issue* 11 (1981).

19. Portia Law School, *Announcements 1925–26* at 12–13. Portia added a day part-time division to its existing evening one in 1920–21. Portia Law School, *Scrapbook 1919–1924,* at 41.

20. *See e.g., The Legacy* (Portia Yearbook), 1939.

21. Articles of Incorporation of Washington College of Law, April 2, 1898.

22. Report of Dean Grace Hays Riley to Washington College of Law Board of Trustees, June 1937.

23. *See* A.Z. Reed, *Present-Day Law Schools* 28 (1928).

24. Auerbach, *supra* note 15, at 76.

25. *See* Robbins, *supra* note 18, at 8.

26. *See* Robbins, *supra* note 18.

27. *Id.,* at 14.

28. Portia Law School, *Scrapbook 1919–1924,* at 115.

29. Boston Herald, March 6, 1929 in *id.* 1928–29 at 92.

30. Letter from Arthur MacLean to Edward H. Deavitt, Chairman, Vermont Board of Bar Examiners, Oct. 17, 1931, at 1.

31. Auerbach, *supra* note 15, at 102.

32. *Id.*

33. Professed concern by the elite bar about the ethical standards of the lawyers graduating from part-time schools was not borne out by the facts. Of 109 lawyers disbarred in Massachusetts from 1900 to 1930, only 6 were from part-time schools, though in 1922 70% of the bar were graduates of such schools, a percentage dropping only to 65% in 1925. 6 Am. L. School Rev. 597 (1930); 5 Am. L. School Rev. 30–31 (1922).

34. Lawrence Tribune, Oct. 7, 1931, in Portia Law School, *Scrapbook 1931–32,* at 27.

35. Boston Morning Globe, Feb. 1, 1932, in Portia Law School, *Scrapbook 1931–32,* at 48. An example of Archer's ire can be found in his book *The Educational Octopus* 275–278 (1915): "The hope of our nation is in the children, especially in the children of the working class man . . . any organization, therefore, whose positive ideal is that the son of the working man should be kept in his place . . . that he should be denied the opportunity to compete with those whose parents could surround them with the advantages and luxuries of life, is an organization inimical to the welfare of the state. . . . Both the men and women who compose this organization are honest in their intentions. . . . Bred as they have been, apart from the struggling masses of humanity . . . they have come to that state of mind that the generations of privilege inevitably bring—the belief in the divine right of the [upper] classes to think for and control the masses. . . . [Wherever] you find them in such places of responsibility, they are not the Harvard progressives, but the Harvard reactionaries, with their contempt for the 'cart horses' as they term the sons of the working man in their belief of the 'divine right' of the lettered aristocracy."

36. Boston Herald, March 17, 1932, in Portia Law School, *Scrapbook 1931–33,* at 55; *see also,* Boston Globe, Mar. 17, 1932, in Portia Law School, *Scrapbook 1931–1933* at 56.

37. *See generally,* J.T. Tinnelly, *Part-time Legal Education: A Study of the Problems of Evening Law Schools* (1957).

38. Boston Post, Feb. 5, 1929, in Portia Law School, *Scrapbook 1928–1929,* at 86.

39. Boston Evening Globe, March 5, 1929, in *id.,* at 91.

40. Boston Traveler, April 20, 1929, in *id.,* at 103.

41. Boston Globe, Dec. 13, 1928 in *id.,* at 73.

42. *See, e.g.,* Robbins, *supra* note 18, at 15. Unlike midwestern states, Massachusetts had no public higher education system at the time from which to draw students, and this was, therefore likely viewed as a necessary step. The two year college requirement did delay the entrance of Portia and Suffolk students into a crowded profession and allowed elite lawyers to pretend that theirs was a unified, rather than stratified bar.

43. Hummer, *supra* note 7, reports 2181 female students enrolled in U.S. law schools in 1928 and 2203 in 1930. Taking 2200 as a round figure for 1929 and 500 as a round figure for Portia enrollment in 1928 (Boston Post, Aug. 11, 1929 in Portia Law School, *Scrapbook 1928–29,* at 138), the Portia figure for 1929 would be 30% higher or 650 (see e.g. Boston Evening Globe, Sept. 21, 1929 in *id.,* at 143). 650 rounds off to 30% of 2200.

44. Notice from Mrs. Alfred Gardner, in Portia Law School, *Scrapbook 1919–20* at 40. *See* "First Women's Law School Opens this Fall," The New York Times, Oct. 3, 1915 *(Magazine).*

45. Letter from Sarah Robinson Frantz (whose husband taught at the school) to Herb Glose, (SUNY Buffalo law student working with the author), Ithaca, N.Y., March 24, 1981.

46. *See e.g.,* Washington College of Law Catalogue 1929–1930, at 8. *See generally,* G. Hathaway, *Fate Rides a Tortoise* (1937), a biography of Mussey.

47. *See, e.g.,* Schade, A History of Washington College of Law, unpublished paper presented for the Masters in Library Science at Catholic University, Washington, D.C., April, 1969.

48. "History of the College," at 1 in *Washington College of Law Archives* (available from Dr. Paul Purta, Director of Development).

49. "Dates to Remember—The History of the Washington College of Law," at 1 in *id.*

50. Dean Grace Hays Riley, Report to WCL Board of Trustees, June, 1937. These figures were arrived at after subtracting drop-outs.

51. Application of Dean Ellen Spencer Mussey, in *Minutes of the Board of Trustees of WCL 1914–[end],* at 52.

52. *See generally,* Washington College of Law, *Scrapbook 1926–1931.*

53. Dean Emma Gillett, Report to WCL Board of Trustees, April 10, 1925.

54. *The College Grit* (WCL student newspaper), Dec. 22, 1933, at 2.

55. *Id.,* April 11, 1935, at 4.

56. *See generally,* Washington College of Law, *Catalogue* 1929–30.

57. Reports of Dean Grace Hays Riley to WCL Board of Trustees, June, 1932 and June, 1937.

58. Report of Dean Grace Hays Riley to WCL Board of Trustees, Dec. 28, 1928.

59. *See* Schade, *supra* note 47.

60. Report of Dean Grace Hays Riley to WCL Board of Trustees, June 4, 1940.

3. BOSTON

1. See J. Auerbach, *Unequal Justice* 58 (1976).

2. *Id.* at 95–96.

3. *Id.* at 95.

4. *See* Robbins, "Opportunity's Haven: The Ambiguous Heritage of Suffolk University Law School," *The Advocate (Suffolk Law School: 75th Anniversary Issue* 11 (1981)

5. Auerbach, *supra* note 1, at 98.

6. Martin, "Night Law Schools," 3 *A.L.S.R.* 454 (Winter, 1914).

7. *Id. See* Auerbach, *supra* note 1.

8. Auerbach, *supra* note 1 at 98–99. Alfred Z. Reed, whom many elite lawyers hoped would recommend closing of the part-time schools, concluded instead in his Carnegie Foundation study *Present-Day Law Schools* (1928) that there was a place for these schools and for the two-tiered bar that they and the university schools created.

9. *Id.* at 99.

10. Richards, "Progress in Legal Education, "AALS, Proc., 15, at 63. *See* Auerbach, *supra* note 1, at 100 and J.T. Tinnelly, *Part-time Legal Education: A Study of the Problems of Evening Law Schools* 6–7 (1957).

11. For a sample of Archer's views *see* Stevens, "Two Cheers for 1870: The American Law School," in D.R. Nolan, ed., *Readings in the History of the American Legal Profession* (1980), which recounts Archer's "Facts and Implications of the College Monopoly of Legal Education," delivered before the Section on Legal Education of the ABA Section on Legal Education, 1929 meeting.

12. The Cambridge (Mass.) Tribune, June 31, 1926, at 12.

13. *See* The Dean's Message, The Legacy (Portia yearbook 1936). Patriarchy in higher education for women basically resulted in giving women an education, but not the same one afforded men. *See* Millett, "The Politics of Sex," in B. Welter ed., *The Woman Question in American History* 162, 169 (1973).

14. *See* The Cambridge Tribune, *supra* note 12.

15. "Boston Woman Lawyer Doesn't Want Equal Rights—No Sirree!" unidentified news clipping in Portia Law School, *Scrapbook 1928–29,* at 60.

16. Mildred Salerno (pseudonym), letter to the author, summer, 1981, Weymouth, Mass.

17. Marie Paraboschi, letter to the author, summer, 1981, Boston, Mass.

18. Jacqueline Guild Lloyd, interview with Laurie Applefeld, summer, 1981, Boston, Mass.

19. Sarah Wallace, interview with Laurie Applefeld, summer, 1981, Boston, Mass.

20. One serious student whom Sara evidently did not know about was Eleanor Wyllys Allen, who, after graduating from Radcliffe College in 1918, attended Yale University, the University of Brussels, and Radcliffe again until 1923, when she was awarded a Ph.D. in international law. Allen entered Portia in 1925–26 while employed at the Harvard Law Library and living at home with her mother on Commonwealth Avenue in Boston. Slightly out of phase with Sara's program, Eleanor graduated from Portia in January, rather than June, 1930. Three years after her Portia graduation she published a nationally recognized book, *The Position of Foreign States before National Courts*, and was for many years curator of the Olivart Collection of International Law at Harvard Law School. *See* student file of Eleanor W. Allen, New England School of Law, Registrar's Office.

21. Gladys Shapiro, interview with the author, summer, 1981, Boston, Mass.

22. Helene Lawrence, interview with Laurie Applefeld, summer 1981, Boston, Mass.

23. Grace Minton O'Hare, interview with Laurie Applefeld, summer 1981, Boston, Mass.

24. Charlotte Slavit, interview with Laurie Applefeld, summer 1981, Boston, Mass.

25. These conclusions are based on the remarks of Prof. Geraldine Clifford of the University of California, Berkeley, during a colloquium at Radcliffe College, Cambridge, Mass. in Spring, 1982.

4. WASHINGTON

1. For a short biography, *see* "Alice Paul," 63 *Wom. L.J.* 131 (1977).

2. *See* Sue White, Papers, Schlesinger Library on the History of Women in America, Radcliffe College, Cambridge, Mass.

3. *See* Statement of Dean Elizabeth Harris to WCL Board of Trustees, May 29, 1924.

4. The Washington Daily News, November 14, 1931, at 15.

5. In 1935, 110 women passed the exam for junior attorney, 6 for associate attorney, and 1 for senior attorney. These and the figures cited in text are from U.S. Civil Service Commission, 47th Annual Report 63 (1938).

6. *See, e.g.,* Millhouse, "Career Seekers Advised to Study Technicalities" Washington Post, November 13, 1935, at 15, col. 6.

7. *See, e.g.,* "Women Regard Lawyer Debate with Tolerance," unidentified Washington newspaper, March 28, 1934, Schlesinger Library, *supra* note 2.

8. Burnita Shelton Matthews, papers, Schlesinger Library, *supra* note 2.

9. About Willebrandt and Adams, *see* Philadelphia Record, Oct. 28, 1934, at 135.

10. Annabel Matthews, Papers, Box 1, Folder 16, Schlesinger Library, *supra* note 2.

11. Maude Pryse, interview with the author, May, 1982, Washington, D.C.

12. Janet Morgan (pseudonym), interview with Ann E. Rascati, June 1982, Fairfax, Va.

13. Elizabeth Salisbury Denny, interview with the author, May 1982, Washington, D.C.

14. Marguerite Rawalt, interview with Ann E. Rascati, June 1982, Washington, D.C.

15. Nadine Gallagher, interview with Ann E. Rascati, June 1982, Easton, Md.

5. CHICAGO

1. Barnes, "Women and Entrance to the Legal Profession," 23 *J. Leg. Ed.* 276 (1971).

2. *See* C. Bird, *Enterprising Women* 108 (1976).

3. *In re Bradwell,* 55 Ill. 535, 538 (1870).

4. *Bradwell v. State,* 83 U.S. 130 (1872).

5. 83 U.S. at 141.

6. Bird, *supra* note 2, at 108, 110.

7. "History of the Chicago-Kent College of Law," *The Transcript* (Yearbook) 10–11 (1925).

8. *Id.* at 11.

9. *Id.* at 11–12.

10. *Id.* at 11.

11. *The Transcript* 98 (1920).

12. *The Transcript* 49 (1922).

13. 1 *Chi.-Kent Rev.* 12 (March, 1923).

14. 1 *Chi.-Kent Rev.* 12 (April, 1923).

15. 5 *Chi.-Kent Rev.* 3 (April, 1927).

16. 6 *Chi.-Kent Rev.* 21 (Nov., 1927).

17. *Id.* at 24.

18. 9 *Chi.-Kent Rev.* 147 (1930).

19. 11 *Chi.-Kent Rev.* 62 (1932).

20. 7 *Chi.-Kent Rev.* 9 (Jan. 1928).

21. *The Transcript* 36 (1936).

22. *Id.* at 41.

23. *Id.* at 35.

24. *Id.* at 28.

25. *Id.* at 84.

26. *The Transcript* 55 (1921).

27. *The Transcript* 29 (1924).

28. *The Transcript* 48 (1927).

29. *The Transcript* 72 (1929).

30. M. Viner, "Co-Education in Law," *The Transcript* 136 (1925).

31. *Id.*

32. *Id.* at 137–139.

33. *Id.* at 139.

34. *Id.*

35. *Id.*

36. *Id.*

37. *Id.*

38. I. Adden, "Why Women Should Study Law," 1 *Chi.-Kent Rev.* 12 (May, 1923).

39. *Id.*

40. *Id.*

41. Blanche Aronin Lippitz, interview with the author, July, 1982, Chicago, Ill.

42. Edna Cronin Smith (pseudonym), interview with the author, July, 1982, Chicago, Ill.

43. Sabra Stein (pseudonym), interview with the author, July, 1982, Chicago, Ill.

44. Liberty Dvorak, interview with the author, July, 1982, Chicago, Ill.

45. Edith Renier Johnson, interview with the author, July, 1982, Chicago, Ill.

6. CONCLUSION

1. Lerner, "The Challenges of Women's History," in Assoc. of Am. Colleges, *Liberal Education and the New Scholarship on Women* (Association of American Colleges, Report of the Wingspread Conference) 40 (1982).

2. *Id.*

3. See Epstein, "Law Partners and Marital Partners," 24 *Human Relations* no. 6 549 (1971).

4. For a complaint by a feminist in her 30's that the young professional women in their 20's no longer think of themselves as women first and professionals second, *see* Bolotin, "Voices from the Post-Feminist Generation," The New York Times, October 17, 1982, (Magazine) at 28.

5. M. Harrison, *A Woman in Residence* (1982).

6. *See* Degler, "The Changing Place of Women in America," in B. Welter ed., *The Woman Question in American History* 133, 140–141 (1973).

Appendix

Sample Interview Format

As you know, we are interested in finding out about the entry of women into the legal profession—and we are particularly interested in the experiences of women like yourself who were in law school in the '20's and '30's.

1. I would first like to know something about your background—
   Could you say a little bit about where you grew up?
   What was your early schooling like?
   Did you go to college? What sort of college was it?
   And your parents?
   What was their educational background?
   Were they born in this country?
   And your grandparents, were they born in this country?
   What did your father do?
   Your mother?
   Any brothers and sisters?
   What did your parents expect you to do in life?
   How did they react to your going to law school?

2. What led up to your decision to go to law school?
   Were there particular individuals that influenced your decision? (Either in childhood, high school or college?)
   Were there particular experiences that influenced your decision? (i.e. certain courses, books, personal experiences)
   Did you consider other alternatives to going to law school? (If "always knew" she would be a lawyer, when did she start to feel that way?) If alternatives—how did you decide between them?
   Did you feel you were unusual in deciding to go to law school?

3. What did you think law school would be like?
    Was it what you expected?
    Can you describe the method of instruction?
    What was a typical week like? (time of classes, number of classes)

4. I would like to get an idea of what your life as a law student was like. Could you describe your school life for me?
    What did your classrooms look like?
    What were your teachers like?
    Do any stand out? (Get names: spellings; if they cannot remember, ask what subject he/she taught)
    What did they expect you to do after law school?
    Were there any women professors (unless this was already indicated)?
    Was there any difference in approach by male or female teachers?
    Did you belong to any social clubs while in school?
    Did you have close friends there? (names, spellings)
    Do you still keep in touch with them?

5. What did you do after graduating?
    Could you tell me a little about your experience taking the bar?
    How did you decide to take the bar? (i.e. was that a goal or plan you held throughout law school)?

(FOR THOSE WHO GOT A JOB):

6. How difficult was it for you to find a job?
    Was it more difficult than you expected?
    What effect did W.W. II have on your job search?

7. Now I would like to get a general sense of what your life after law school was like.
    Could you give me a description of the jobs that you held and the kind of work you did? If you changed jobs, why did you decide to do that? For each change—Did your being a woman affect how you were treated in this job?
    Were you married during this time?
    Did you have children?
    (If Yes): How did you manage to combine your work life and your home life?
    (If No): Did you consider getting married or did you feel it would interfere with your career?

Index

©Cheri Hoyt

About the author

Ronald Chester is Professor of Law at New England School of Law in Boston. He graduated from Harvard, Columbia, and Cambridge Universities. He has previously treated equal opportunity issues in *Inheritance, Wealth, and Society* (Indiana, 1982) and in a number of published articles. He, his wife Nia, and their two sons Caben and Ian live in Cambridge, Mass.

Related Books from Bergin & Garvey

Families & Change
Social Needs and Public Policy
Rosalie G. Genovese
Foreword by Jessie Bernard

In Her Prime
A New View of Middle-Aged Women
Judith K. Brown and Virginia Kerns
Foreword by Beatrice Blyth Whiting

Househusbands
Men and Housework in American Families
William R. Beer

Women, Work, and Revolution in Latin America
June Nash and Helen Safa

Women's Work
Development and the Division of Labor by Sex
Eleanor Leacock and Helen Safa

Immaculate Deception
A New View of Women and Childbirth
Suzanne Arms
Foreword by Frederick Leboyer

Women and Colonization
Anthropological Perspectives
Mona Etienne and Eleanor Leacock

Women and Nutrition in Third World Countries
Sahni Hamilton, Barry Popkin, and Deborah Spicer

Silent Knife
Cesarean Prevention and Vaginal Birth After Cesarean
Nancy Wainer Cohen and Lois J. Estner

The Trials & Tribulations of Little Red Riding Hood
Versions of the Tale in Sociocultural Context
Jack Zipes

Circumcision
The Painful Dilemma
Rosemary Romberg

Ended Beginnings
Healing Childbearing Losses
Claudia Panuthos and Catherine Romeo
Foreword by Peggy O'Mara McMahon

Boys & Girls at Play
The Development of Sex Roles
Evelyn Pitcher and Lynn Schultz

Women and Men as Leaders
In Business, Educational, and Social Service Organizations
Trudy Heller
Foreword by Lois Hart

Bergin & Garvey Publishers, Inc.
670 Amherst Road
South Hadley, Massachusetts 01075